WINDOWS® 7
Simplified®

Visual

by Paul McFedries

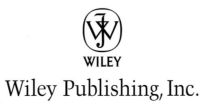

WILEY

Wiley Publishing, Inc.

WINDOWS® 7 SIMPLIFIED®

Published by
Wiley Publishing, Inc.
10475 Crosspoint Boulevard
Indianapolis, IN 46256

www.wiley.com

Published simultaneously in Canada

Library of Congress Control Number: 2009933755

ISBN: 978-0-470-50387-4

Manufactured in the United States of America

10 9 8 7 6

Trademark Acknowledgments

Contact Us

For general information on our other products and services please contact our Customer Care Department within the U.S. at 877-762-2974, outside the U.S. at 317-572-3993 or fax 317-572-4002.

For technical support please visit www.wiley.com/techsupport.

Permissions

Corbis Digital Stock
Digital Vision
PhotoDisc/Getty Images
Purestock

WILEY
Wiley Publishing, Inc.

Sales

Contact Wiley
at (877) 762-2974 or
fax (317) 572-4002.

Praise for Visual Books

"Like a lot of other people, I understand things best when I see them visually. Your books really make learning easy and life more fun."

John T. Frey (Cadillac, MI)

"I have quite a few of your Visual books and have been very pleased with all of them. I love the way the lessons are presented!"

Mary Jane Newman (Yorba Linda, CA)

"I just purchased my third Visual book (my first two are dog-eared now!), and, once again, your product has surpassed my expectations."

Tracey Moore (Memphis, TN)

"I am an avid fan of your Visual books. If I need to learn anything, I just buy one of your books and learn the topic in no time. Wonders! I have even trained my friends to give me Visual books as gifts."

Illona Bergstrom (Aventura, FL)

"Thank you for making it so clear. I appreciate it. I will buy many more Visual books."

J.P. Sangdong (North York, Ontario, Canada)

"I have several books from the Visual series and have always found them to be valuable resources."

Stephen P. Miller (Ballston Spa, NY)

"Thank you for the wonderful books you produce. It wasn't until I was an adult that I discovered how I learn — visually. Nothing compares to Visual books. I love the simple layout. I can just grab a book and use it at my computer, lesson by lesson. And I understand the material! You really know the way I think and learn. Thanks so much!"

Stacey Han (Avondale, AZ)

"I absolutely admire your company's work. Your books are terrific. The format is perfect, especially for visual learners like me. Keep them coming!"

Frederick A. Taylor, Jr. (New Port Richey, FL)

"I have several of your Visual books and they are the best I have ever used."

Stanley Clark (Crawfordville, FL)

"I bought my first Visual book last month. Wow. Now I want to learn everything in this easy format!"

Tom Vial (New York, NY)

"Thank you, thank you, thank you...for making it so easy for me to break into this high-tech world. I now own four of your books. I recommend them to anyone who is a beginner like myself."

Gay O'Donnell (Calgary, Alberta, Canada)

"I write to extend my thanks and appreciation for your books. They are clear, easy to follow, and straight to the point. Keep up the good work! I bought several of your books and they are just right! No regrets! I will always buy your books because they are the best."

Seward Kollie (Dakar, Senegal)

"Compliments to the chef!! Your books are extraordinary! Or, simply put, extra-ordinary, meaning way above the rest! THANK YOU THANK YOU THANK YOU! I buy them for friends, family, and colleagues."

Christine J. Manfrin (Castle Rock, CO)

"What fantastic teaching books you have produced! Congratulations to you and your staff. You deserve the Nobel Prize in Education in the Software category. Thanks for helping me understand computers."

Bruno Tonon (Melbourne, Australia)

"Over time, I have bought a number of your 'Read Less - Learn More' books. For me, they are THE way to learn anything easily. I learn easiest using your method of teaching."

José A. Mazón (Cuba, NY)

"I am an avid purchaser and reader of the Visual series, and they are the greatest computer books I've seen. The Visual books are perfect for people like myself who enjoy the computer, but want to know how to use it more efficiently. Your books have definitely given me a greater understanding of my computer, and have taught me to use it more effectively. Thank you very much for the hard work, effort, and dedication that you put into this series."

Alex Diaz (Las Vegas, NV)

Credits

About the Author

Paul McFedries is a full-time technical writer. Paul has been authoring computer books since 1991 and he has more than 60 books to his credit. Paul's books have sold more than three million copies worldwide. These books include the Wiley titles *Windows 7 Visual Quick Tips*, *Switching to a Mac Portable Genius*, *iPhone 3G Portable Genius*, *Teach Yourself VISUALLY Office 2008 for Mac*, and *Internet Simplified*. Paul is also the proprietor of Word Spy (www.wordspy.com and twitter.com/wordspy), a Web site that tracks new words and phrases as they enter the language. Paul invites you to drop by his personal Web site at www.mcfedries.com, or to follow him on Twitter at twitter.com/paulmcf.

Author's Acknowledgments

It goes without saying that writers focus on text, and I certainly enjoyed focusing on the text that you'll read in this book. However, this book is more than just the usual collection of words and phrases. A quick thumb-through of the pages will show you that this book is also chock full of images, from sharp screen shots to fun and informative illustrations. Those colorful images sure make for a beautiful book, and that beauty comes from a lot of hard work by Wiley's immensely talented group of designers and layout artists. They are all listed in the Credits section on the previous page, and I thank them for creating another gem. Of course, what you read in this book must also be accurate, logically presented, and free of errors. Ensuring all of this was an excellent group of editors that included project editor Sarah Hellert, copy editor Scott Tullis, and technical editor Vince Averello. Thanks to all of you for your exceptional competence and hard work. Thanks, as well, to acquisitions editor Jody Lefevere for asking me to write this book.

Table of Contents

1

Getting Started with Windows

2

Launching and Working with Programs

Creating and Editing Documents

Working with Images

Table of Contents

Playing Music and Other Media

Working with Files

Sharing Your Computer with Others

Surfing the World Wide Web

Table of Contents

9

Working with E-mail, Contacts, and Events

10

Implementing Security in Windows 7

Customizing Windows 7

Maintaining Windows 7

How to Use This Book

Do you look at the pictures in a book or newspaper before anything else on a page? Would you rather see an image instead of read about how to do something? Search no further. This book is for you. Opening Windows 7 Simplified allows you to read less and learn more about the Windows operating system.

Who Needs This Book

This book is for a reader who has never used this particular technology or application. It is also for more computer literate individuals who want to expand their knowledge of the different features that Windows has to offer.

Book Organization

Windows 7 Simplified has 12 chapters.

Chapter 1, **Getting Started with Windows 7**, gives you the basics of starting and stopping Windows 7, understanding the Windows 7 screen, and using a mouse.

In Chapter 2, **Launching and Working with Programs**, you learn how to install and start programs, how to use menus, toolbars, and dialog boxes, and how to switch between program windows.

In Chapter 3, **Creating and Editing Documents**, you learn how to create and open documents, edit document text, and save and print your work.

Chapter 4, **Working with Images**, shows you how to work with images in Windows 7, load images from the digital camera or scanner, and print an image.

With Chapter 5, **Playing Music and Other Media**, you learn how to use Windows Media Player to play music, sound, and video files, audio CDs, and DVDs.

Chapter 6, **Working with Files**, gives you the details on how to view, select, copy, and move files, burn files to a recordable CD, rename and delete files, and search for files.

Chapter 7, **Sharing Your Computer with Others**, shows you how to use Windows 7's User Accounts feature to enable multiple people to share a single computer, and introduces you to some basic networking techniques.

In Chapter 8, **Surfing the World Wide Web**, you learn how to use the Internet Explorer program to browse the World Wide Web.

With Chapter 9, **Working with E-mail, Contacts, and Events**, you learn how to use the Windows Live Mail program to send and receive e-mail messages and track your appointments, events, and tasks.

Chapter 10, **Implementing Security in Windows 7**, gives you information on the Windows 7 security features, including the new Action Center, passwords, parental controls, and more.

Chapter 11, **Customizing Windows 7**, shows you various ways to customize Windows 7 to suit the way you work.

In Chapter 12, **Maintaining Windows 7**, you learn about some programs that enable you to perform routine maintenance that will keep your system running smoothly.

Chapter Organization

This book consists of sections, all listed in the book's table of contents. A section is a set of steps that show you how to complete a specific computer task.

Each section, usually contained on two facing pages, has an introduction to the task at hand, a set of full-color screen shots and steps that walk you through the task, and a set of tips. This format allows you to quickly look at a topic of interest and learn it instantly.

Chapters group together three or more sections with a common theme. A chapter may also contain pages that give you the background information needed to understand the sections in a chapter.

Using the Mouse

This book uses the following conventions to describe the actions you perform when using the mouse:

Click

Press your left mouse button once. You generally click your mouse on something to select something on the screen.

Double-click

Press your left mouse button twice. Double-clicking something on the computer screen generally opens whatever item you have double-clicked.

Right-click

Press your right mouse button. When you right-click anything on the computer screen, the program displays a shortcut menu containing commands specific to the selected item.

Click and Drag, and Release the Mouse

Move your mouse pointer and hover it over an item on the screen. Press and hold down the left mouse button. Now, move the mouse to where you want to place the item and then release the button. You use this method to move an item from one area of the computer screen to another.

The Conventions in This Book

A number of typographic and layout styles have been used throughout *Windows 7 Simplified* to distinguish different types of information.

Bold

Bold type represents the names of commands and options that you interact with. Bold type also indicates text and numbers that you must type into a dialog box or window.

Italics

Italic words introduce a new term and are followed by a definition.

Numbered Steps

You must perform the instructions in numbered steps in order to successfully complete a section and achieve the final results.

Bulleted Steps

These steps point out various optional features. You do not have to perform these steps; they simply give additional information about a feature. Steps without bullets tell you what the program does in response to your following a numbered step. For example, if you click a menu command, a dialog box may appear or a window may open. The step text may also tell you what the final result is when you follow a set of numbered steps.

Notes

Notes give additional information. They may describe special conditions that may occur during an operation. They may warn you of a situation that you want to avoid — for example, the loss of data. A note may also cross reference a related area of the book. A cross reference may guide you to another chapter or another section within the current chapter.

Icons and buttons

Icons and buttons are graphical representations within the text. They show you exactly what you need to click to perform a step.

 You can easily identify the tips in any section by looking for the Simplify It icon. Tips offer additional information, including tips, hints, and tricks. You can use the tip information to go beyond what you have learned in the steps.

Chapter 1

Getting Started with Windows 7

Are you ready to learn about Windows 7? In this chapter, you learn a few basic techniques and concepts that will help get comfortable with Windows. These topics include starting Windows 7, understanding what you can do with Windows 7, and taking a tour of the Windows 7 screen. You also learn how to use a mouse with Windows 7, use the Windows 7 Help system, and activate your copy of Windows 7. The chapter closes by showing you how to restart Windows 7 and how to shut down your system when you are finished using it.

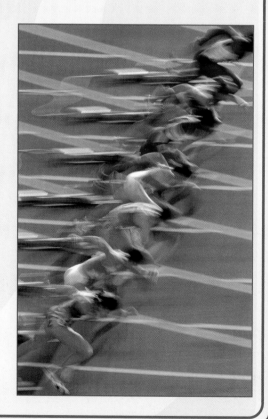

Start
Windows 7

When you turn on your computer, Windows 7 starts automatically, but you may have to navigate the Welcome screen along the way. You use the Welcome screen to log in to Windows 7 using the user account and password you configured when you first set up your computer.

If this is the first time you are starting your computer, you will have to run through a series of configuration steps. These steps configure your main user account, your desktop background, and a few security options. You should select the default options to ensure your computer remains secure and up to date.

Start Windows 7

① Turn on your computer.

● The Windows 7 Welcome screen appears.

Note: *If your version of Windows 7 is configured with just a single user and no password, then you bypass the Welcome screen and go directly to the desktop.*

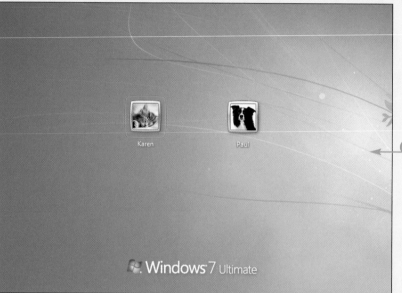

② Click the icon that corresponds to your Windows 7 user name.

Windows 7 prompts you to enter your password.

Note: *If you are the only user on your computer, Windows 7 prompts you for your password right away, so you can skip Step 2.*

③ Type your password.

Note: *The password characters appear as dots as you type them so that no one else can read your password.*

Paul

Switch User

Windows 7 Ultimate

④ Click the **Go** arrow (⊙) or press `Enter`.

The Windows 7 desktop appears after a few moments.

Paul

Switch User

Windows 7 Ultimate

Simplify It

What happens if I forget my Windows 7 password?
Most Windows 7 user accounts that are password protected are also set up with a password *hint* — usually a word or phrase designed to jog your memory. You choose the question when you set your password, as explained in the "Protect an Account with a Password" section in Chapter 10. If you forget your password, click the **Go** arrow (⊙) and then click **OK** to see the password hint.

What You Can Do with Windows 7

Windows 7 is an operating system that contains a collection of tools, programs, and resources. You do not do anything directly with Windows 7 itself. Instead, you use its tools and programs to perform tasks, including getting your work done, creating pictures, editing photos, playing music, surfing the World Wide Web, exchanging e-mail messages, and more. Here is a sampling of what you can do with them.

Get Work Done

With Windows 7, you can run programs that enable you to get your work done more efficiently, such as a word processor for writing memos and letters, a spreadsheet for making calculations, and a database for storing information. Windows 7 comes with some of these programs (such as the WordPad program you learn about in Chapter 3), and you can purchase and install others separately.

Create and Edit Pictures

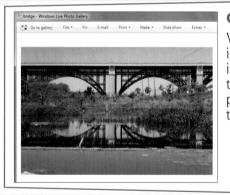

Windows 7 comes with a lot of features that let you work with images. You can create your own pictures from scratch, import images from a scanner or digital camera, or download images from the Internet. After you create or acquire an image, you can edit it, print it, or send it via e-mail. You learn about these and other picture tasks in Chapter 4.

Play Music and Other Media

Windows 7 has treats for your ears as well as your eyes. You can listen to audio CDs, play digital sound and video clips, watch DVD movies, tune in to Internet radio stations, and copy audio files to a recordable CD. You learn about these multimedia tasks in Chapter 5.

Get on the Internet

Windows 7 makes connecting to the Internet easy. And after you are on the Net, Windows 7 has all the tools you need to get the most out of your experience. For example, you can use Internet Explorer to surf the World Wide Web (see Chapter 8) and Windows Live Mail to send and receive e-mail (see Chapter 9).

The Windows 7 Screen

Before getting to the specifics of working with Windows 7, take a few seconds to familiarize yourself with the basic screen elements, including the desktop, the Start button, the taskbar, and the notification area. You will interact with these screen elements throughout your Windows 7 career, so getting familiar with them early on will help you in the long run.

Desktop Icon

An icon on the desktop represents a program, a Windows 7 feature, or a document. A program you install often adds its own icon on the desktop.

Mouse Pointer

When you move your mouse, this pointer moves along with it.

Desktop

This is the Windows 7 "work area," meaning that it is where you work with your programs and documents.

Time and Date

This is the current time and date on your computer. To see the full date, position the mouse ⌖ over the time. To change the date or time, click the time.

Notification Area

This area displays small icons that notify you about things that are happening on your computer. For example, you see notifications if your printer runs out of paper or if an update to Windows 7 is available over the Internet.

Taskbar

The programs you have open appear in the taskbar. You use this area to switch between programs if you have more than one running at a time.

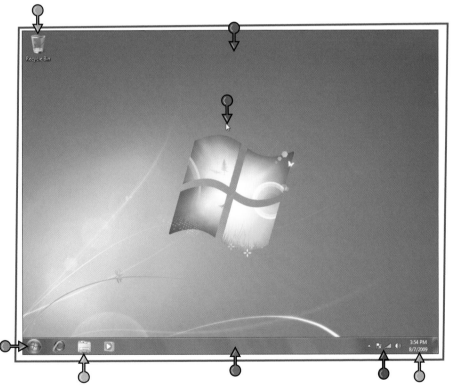

Start Button

You use this button to start programs and launch many of Windows 7's features.

Taskbar Icons

You use these icons to launch some Windows 7 features with just a mouse click.

Using a Mouse with Windows 7

Windows 7 was built with the mouse in mind, so it pays to learn the basic mouse techniques early on because you will use them for as long as you use Windows. These techniques include clicking the mouse, double-clicking, right-clicking, and clicking-and-dragging.

If you have never used a mouse before, remember to keep all your movements slow and deliberate, and practice the techniques in this section as much as you can.

Using a Mouse with Windows 7

CLICK THE MOUSE

① Position the mouse ⬚ over the object you want to work with.

② Click the left mouse button.

● Depending on the object, Windows 7 either selects the object or performs some operation in response to the click (such as displaying the Start menu).

DOUBLE-CLICK THE MOUSE

① Position the mouse ⬚ over the object you want to work with.

② Click the left mouse button twice in quick succession.

● Windows 7 usually performs some operation in response to the double-click action (such as displaying the Recycle Bin window).

RIGHT-CLICK THE MOUSE

1 Position the mouse ▷ over the object you want to work with.

2 Click the right mouse button.

● Windows 7 displays a shortcut menu when you right-click something.

Note: The contents of the shortcut menu depend on the object you right-clicked.

CLICK AND DRAG THE MOUSE

1 Position the mouse ▷ over the object you want to work with.

2 Click and hold the left mouse button.

3 Move the mouse to drag the selected object.

● In most cases, the object moves along with the mouse ▷.

4 Release the mouse button when the selected object is repositioned.

Simplify It

Why does Windows 7 sometimes not recognize my double-clicks?
Try to double-click as quickly as you can, and be sure not to move the mouse between clicks. If you continue to have trouble, click **Start**, **Control Panel**, **Hardware and Sound**, and then **Mouse** to open the Mouse Properties dialog box. Click the **Buttons** tab. In the Double-click Speed group, click and drag the slider to the left (toward Slow).

How can I set up my mouse for a left-hander?
Click **Start**, **Control Panel**, **Hardware and Sound**, and then **Mouse** to open the Mouse Properties dialog box. Click the **Buttons** tab. Click **Switch primary and secondary buttons** (☐ changes to ☑).

Get Help

You can find out more about Windows 7, learn how to perform a task, or troubleshoot problems by accessing the Window 7 Help and Support system.

Most of the Windows 7 Help and Support system is arranged into various categories, such as "Security and privacy" and "Files, folders, and libraries." Each category offers a number of subcategories to help you find the specific area you are looking for. Within each category and subcategory you see a collection of related topics, and these topics provide the instructions of information.

Get Help

① Click **Start**.

The Start menu appears.

② Click **Help and Support**.

The Windows Help and Support window appears.

③ Click the **Browse Help** button (🔲).

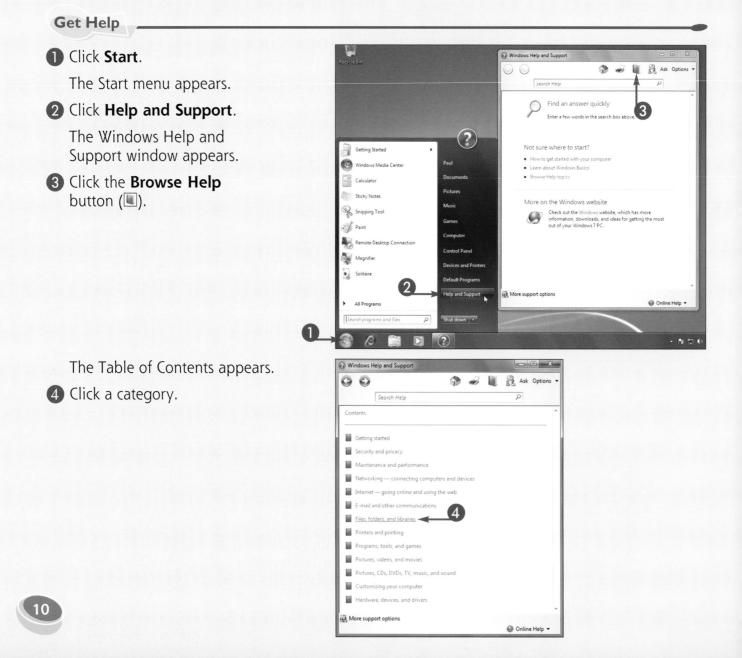

The Table of Contents appears.

④ Click a category.

⬤ A list of Help topics appears for the category you selected.

⬤ A list of subcategories appears for the category you selected.

5 Click a topic.

Note: *If the topic you want is part of a subcategory, click the subcategory to display the list of topics it contains, and then click the topic.*

⬤ The item you selected appears in the Windows Help and Support Center window.

6 Read the article.

Note: *To return to a previous Windows Help and Support Center screen, click the **Back** button (⬅) until you get to the screen you want.*

Simplify It

How do I get help for a specific program?
Almost all Windows programs have their own Help features. You can access Help in a specific program one of three main ways:

● Click **Help** from the menu, and then click the command that runs the Help features (it may be called **Help Contents**, **Help Topics**, or *Program* **Help**, where *Program* is the name of the program (for example, **Microsoft Word Help**).

● Press [F1].

● In a dialog box or program window, click the **Help** button (⬚).

Activate Your Copy of Windows 7

To avoid piracy, Microsoft requires that each copy of Windows 7 be activated. Otherwise, your copy of Windows 7 will refuse to run after the activation period has expired. Activating Windows 7 means that Microsoft uses an Internet connection to confirm that your copy of Windows 7 is genuine and has not also been installed on another computer.

This section assumes that Windows 7 has not yet prompted you to start the activation. If you see an icon in the notification area with the message "Activate Windows now," click that message and then skip to Step 5.

Activate Your Copy of Windows 7

1 Click **Start**.

The Start menu appears.

2 Right-click **Computer**.

3 Click **Properties**.

The System window appears.

Note: *If the System window shows the Ask for Genuine Microsoft Software logo in the Windows Activation area, then you do not need to perform the rest of the steps in this section. Click the* **Close** *button (⊠) to close the System window.*

4 Click the **Activate Windows now** link.

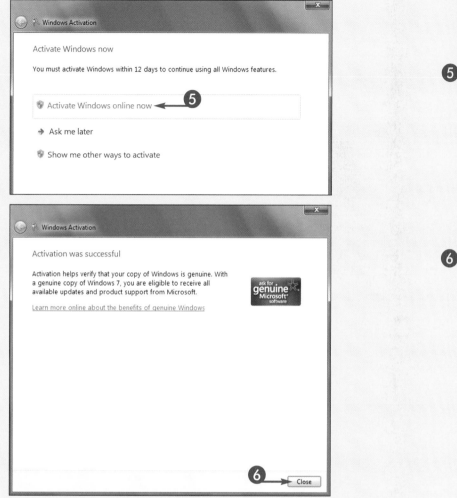

The Windows Activation dialog box appears.

5 Click **Activate Windows online now**.

Windows 7 confirms that it has been activated.

6 Click **Close**.

Can I activate Windows 7 on more than one computer?
No, not usually. The activation process creates a special value unique to your computer's hardware configuration. When you activate Windows 7, your copy of the program is associated with this unique hardware value, which means your copy works only with that one computer. However, if that computer breaks down, you can telephone Microsoft to let them know, and they should allow you to activate Windows 7 on another computer.

How can I activate my copy of Windows 7 if I do not have Internet access?
If you do not have Internet access, perform Steps **1** to **5** anyway. After a few moments, Windows Activation displays a list of options. Click **Show me other ways to activate**. If your computer has a modem attached, click **Use my modem to connect directly to the activation service**. If you do not have a modem, click **Use the automated phone system**, instead.

Restart Windows 7

You can restart Windows 7, which means it shuts down and starts up again immediately. This is useful if your computer is running slow or acting funny. Sometimes a restart solves the problem.

Knowing how to restart Windows 7 also comes in handy when you install a program or device that requires a restart to function properly. If you are busy right now, you can always opt to restart your computer yourself later, when it is more convenient.

Restart Windows 7

① Shut down all your running programs.

Note: *Be sure to save your work as you close your programs.*

② Click **Start**.

The Start menu appears.

③ Click the power button arrow (▶).

④ Click **Restart**.

Windows 7 shuts down and your computer restarts.

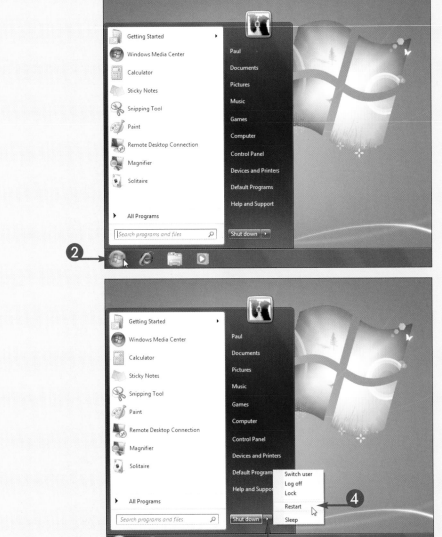

Shut Down Windows 7

When you complete your work for the day, you should shut down Windows 7. However, do not just shut off your computer's power. Follow the proper steps to avoid damaging files on your system.

Shutting off the computer's power without properly exiting Windows 7 can cause two problems. First, if you have unsaved changes in some open documents, you may lose those changes. Second, you could damage one or more Windows 7 system files, which could make your system unstable.

Shut Down Windows 7

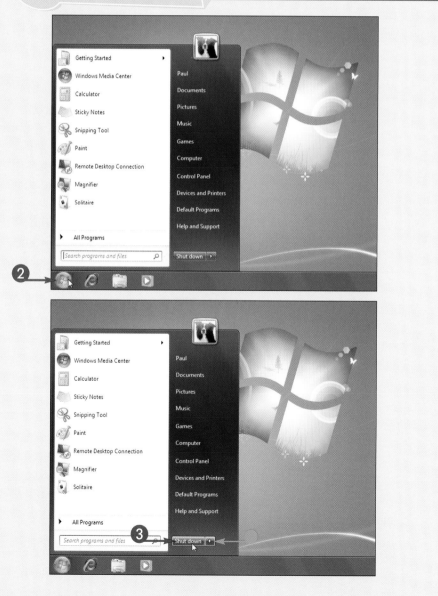

① Shut down all your running programs.

Note: *Be sure to save your work as you close your programs.*

② Click **Start**.

The Start menu appears.

③ Click **Shut Down**.

Windows 7 shuts down and turns off your computer.

● If you want Windows 7 to automatically reopen all the programs and documents currently on your screen, click the power button arrow (▶) and then click **Sleep**, instead.

Chapter 2

Launching and Working with Programs

On its own, Windows 7 does not do very much. To do something useful with your computer, you need to work with a program, which at first will probably mean a program that comes with Windows 7, which offers a number of useful programs.

However, you can also work with any program that you install yourself, and this chapter shows you how to install programs.

In this chapter you also learn how to launch programs, understand program windows, and work with program pull-down menus, toolbars, dialog boxes, scrollbars, and jump lists.

Install a Program

If Windows 7 does not come with a program that you need, you can obtain the program yourself, either from a computer store or via an Internet download. You can then install the program on your computer.

How you start the installation process depends on what format the program comes in. If you purchased the program from a store, then the program comes on a **CD** or **DVD** disc, and you use that disc to install the program. On the other hand, if you downloaded the program from the Internet, the program comes on the downloaded file, and you use that file to install the program.

Install a Program

INSTALL FROM A CD OR DVD

1 Insert the program's disc into your computer's CD or DVD drive.

● The AutoPlay dialog box appears.

2 Click **Run** *file*, where *file* is the name of the installation program (usually SETUP.EXE).

3 Follow the installation instructions the program provides.

Note: *Installation steps vary from program to program.*

INSTALL FROM A FILE DOWNLOADED FROM THE INTERNET

1 Click **Start**.

2 Type **downloads**.

3 Click **Downloads**.

Note: If you saved the downloaded file in a folder other than Downloads, use Windows Explorer to find the downloaded file. To view a file with Windows Explorer, see the "View Your Files" section in Chapter 6.

The Downloads folder appears.

4 Double-click the file.

The software's installation program begins.

Note: For compressed files, extract the files, and then double-click the setup file.

5 Follow the installation instructions the program provides.

Simplify It

How do I find my software's product key or serial number?
The product key or serial number is crucial because many programs do not install until you enter the number. Look for a sticker attached to the back or inside of the CD case. Also look on the registration card, the CD itself, or the back of the box. If you downloaded the program, the number should appear on the download screen and on the e-mail receipt you receive.

Change or Repair a Program Installation

When you install a program, you can choose the "custom" installation option to install only some of the program's components. If you decide later to install more components or remove installed components, you can rerun the install program to make these changes.

If an installed program does not start or behaves erratically, it may have one or more missing or corrupt files. Many programs come with a repair option that can fix such problems.

Change or Repair a Program Installation

① Click **Start**.

② Click **Control Panel**.

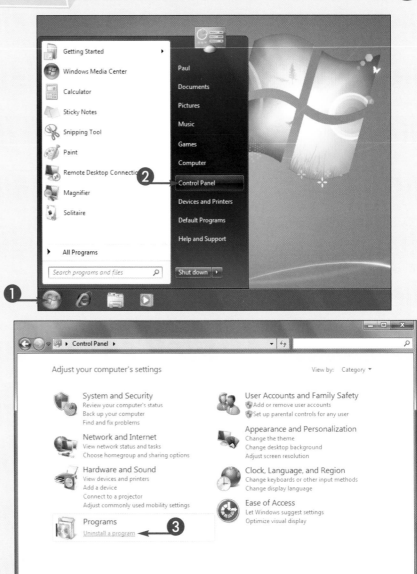

The Control Panel window appears.

③ Click **Uninstall a program**.

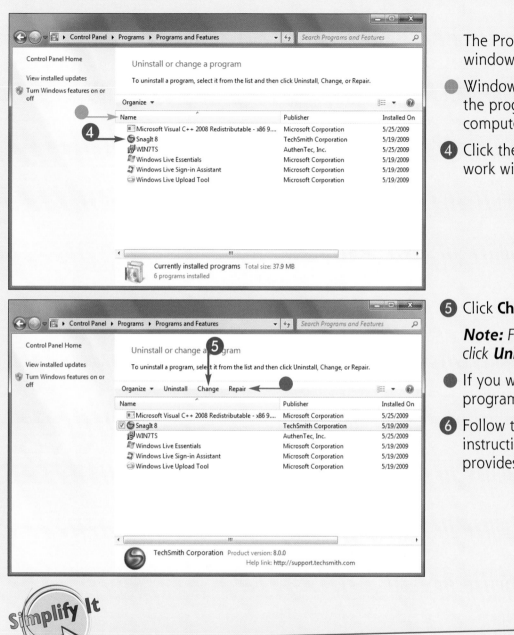

The Programs and Features window appears.

● Windows 7 displays a list of the programs installed on your computer.

④ Click the program you want to work with.

⑤ Click **Change**.

Note: *For some programs, you click **Uninstall/Change**, instead.*

● If you want to repair the program, click **Repair** instead.

⑥ Follow the installation instructions the program provides.

What is the difference between a "typical" and "custom" installation?
A "typical" installation automatically installs only those program components that people use most often. In a "custom" installation, you select which components are installed, where they are installed, and so on. The custom option is best suited for experienced users, so you are usually better off choosing the typical install.

Is it dangerous to repair a program?
Generally speaking, no it is not dangerous to repair a program. In almost all cases, what the repair tool does is copy fresh copies of the program's original files to your hard disk. However, in some rare cases repairing a program could cause you to lose data that you created using the program. For this reason, it is a good idea to back up your data before repairing any program. See Chapter 12 to learn how to perform backups in Windows 7.

Start a Program

To work with any program, you must first tell Windows 7 what program you want to run. You normally do this by selecting the program via the Windows 7 Start menu, which contains a list of the programs you use most often, as well as various submenus that contain icons for all the programs installed on your computer. In Windows 7, you can also use the taskbar to start some programs.

Whichever method you use, Windows 7 then launches the program and displays it on the desktop.

① Click **Start**.

● If the program you want to use has a taskbar button, you can click the button to launch the program.

② Click **All Programs**.

Note: When you click **All Programs**, the command name changes to Back.

③ Click the icon for the program you want to launch.

● If your program icon is in a submenu, click the submenu and then click the program icon.

The program appears on the desktop.

● Windows 7 adds a button for the program to the taskbar.

Note: After you have used a program a few times, it may appear on the main Start menu. If so, you can launch the program by clicking its Start menu icon.

Understanding Program Windows

When you start a program, it appears on the Windows 7 desktop in its own window. You work with a program by manipulating the various features of its window. These features include the title bar, menu bar, toolbar, and three buttons: Minimize, Maximize, and Close.

System Menu Icon

Clicking this icon or pressing `Alt` + `Spacebar` displays a menu that enables you to work with program windows via the keyboard.

Title Bar

The title bar displays the name of the program. In some programs, the title bar also displays the name of the open document. You can also use the title bar to move the window.

Menu Bar

The menu bar contains the pull-down menus for Windows 7 and most Windows 7 software. In some programs you must press `Alt` to see the menu bar.

Toolbar

Buttons that offer easy access to common program commands and features appear in the toolbar. Some buttons are commands and some have lists from which you can make a choice.

Minimize Button

You click the **Minimize** button (🗕) to remove the window from the desktop and display only the window's taskbar button. The window is still open, but not active.

Maximize Button

To enlarge the window either from the taskbar or so that it takes up the entire desktop, you click the **Maximize** button (🗖).

Close Button

When you click the **Close** button (☒), the program shuts down.

Using Pull-Down Menus

When you are ready to work with a program, Windows 7 offers a number of different methods, but the pull-down menus are the most common. You use pull-down menus to access the program's commands and features.

There are two types of items in most pull-down menus: commands that execute some action in the program, or features that you turn on and off.

You access all pull-down menus via the menu bar, and most programs display the menu bar by default. However, if you do not see the menu bar, you can often display it by pressing the **Alt** key.

Using Pull-Down Menus

RUN COMMANDS

1 Click the name of the menu you want to display.

● The program displays the menu.

You can also display a menu by pressing and holding **Alt** and pressing the underlined letter in the menu name.

2 Click the command you want to run.

The program runs the command.

● If your command is in a submenu, click the command.

TURN FEATURES ON AND OFF

1 Click the name of the menu you want to display.

● The program displays the menu.

2 Click the menu item.

● Toggle features are either turned on (indicated by ☑) or off (no check mark appears).

● Click an option feature to turn it on (indicated by ◉) and turn off the previously activated item.

Using Toolbars

You can use a program's toolbars to access commands faster than using the pull-down menus. In most cases, a toolbar is a collection of buttons, lists, or other controls that often give you one-click access to the program's most common features.

Most programs come with one or more toolbars, although in some programs you must first display the toolbar you need. If there is a toolbar that you never use, you can hide it to give yourself more room in the program window.

Using Toolbars

EXECUTE COMMANDS

① Click the toolbar button that represents the command or list.

Note: *If the toolbar button remains "pressed" after you click it, the button toggles a feature on and off and the feature is now on. To turn the feature off, click the button to "unpress" it.*

● The program executes the command or, as shown here, drops down the list.

② If a list appears, click the list item for the command.

The program runs the command.

DISPLAY AND HIDE TOOLBARS

① Click **View**.

② Click **Toolbars**.

③ Click a toolbar.

● If the toolbar is currently displayed (indicated by ☑ in the View menu), the program hides the toolbar.

If the toolbar is currently hidden, the program displays the toolbar (indicated by ☑ in the View menu).

Understanding Dialog Box Controls

When you select some pull-down menu commands or toolbar buttons, the program displays a special window called a dialog box. In some cases, the dialog box displays a message or warning that you need to read. However, most dialog boxes appear when a program needs you to provide information. You provide that information my manipulating various types of controls, including option buttons, check boxes, spin buttons, text boxes, and list boxes.

Option Button

Clicking an option button turns on a program feature. Only one option button in a group can be turned on at a time. When you click an option button, it changes from ⊙ to ◉.

Check Box

Clicking a check box toggles a program feature on and off. If you are turning a feature on, the check box changes from ☐ to ☑; if you are turning the feature off, the check box changes from ☑ to ☐.

Command Button

Clicking a command button executes the command written on the button face. For example, you can click **OK** to put settings you choose in a dialog box into effect and close the dialog box; you can click **Apply** to put the settings into effect and leave the dialog box open; or you can click **Cancel** to close the dialog box without changing the settings.

Tab

The various tabs in a dialog box display different sets of controls. You can choose from these settings in a dialog box to achieve a variety of results.

Spin Button

The spin button (⮝⮟) enables you to choose a numeric value.

Text Box

A text box enables you to enter typed text.

List Box

A list box displays a relatively large number of choices, and you click the item you want. If you do not see the item you want, you can use the scrollbar to bring the item into view; see "Using Scrollbars," later in this chapter.

Combo Box

The combo box combines both a text box and a list box. This means that you can either type the value you want into the text box, or you can use the list to click the value you want.

Drop-Down List Box

A drop-down list box displays only the selected item from a list. You can open the list to select a different item.

Using Dialog Boxes

You use dialog boxes to control how a program works. Dialog boxes appear frequently, so you need to know how to use them to get the most out of any program.

For example, when you print a document, you usually see the Print dialog box, which includes several controls that enable you to control the print job. For example, you might see a list of the available printers, radio buttons that enable you to specify how much of the document you want to print, and a spin button that enables you to specify the number of copies you want printed.

USING A TEXT BOX

1 Click inside the text box.

● A blinking, vertical bar (called a *cursor* or an *insertion point*) appears inside the text box.

2 Use Backspace or Delete to delete any existing characters.

3 Type your text.

ENTER A VALUE WITH A SPIN BUTTON

1 Click the top arrow on the spin button (⬦) to increase the value.

2 Click the bottom arrow on the spin button (⬦) to decrease the value.

● You can also type the value in the text box.

SELECT A LIST BOX ITEM

1 If necessary, click the down arrow (⊡) to scroll down the list and bring the item you want to select into view.

Note: See the "Using Scrollbars" section to learn how to use scrollbars.

2 Click the item.

● Click the up arrow (⊡) to scroll back up through the list.

SELECT AN ITEM USING A COMBO BOX

● Click the item in the list box to select it.

● You can also type the item name in the text box.

SELECT AN ITEM FROM A DROP-DOWN LIST BOX

1 Click the drop-down arrow (⊡).

● The list appears.

2 Click the item in the list that you want to select.

Simplify It

Are there keyboard shortcuts I can use to make dialog boxes easier to work with?

Enter	Selects the default command button (which is indicated with a highlight around it).
Esc	Cancels the dialog box (which is the same as clicking **Cancel**).
Alt + *letter*	Selects the control that has the *letter* underlined.
Tab	Moves forward through the dialog box controls.
Shift + Tab	Moves backward through the dialog box controls.
⬆ and ⬇	Moves up and down within the current option button group.
Alt + ⬇	Drops down the selected combo box or drop-down list box.

Work with Program Windows

You need to know how to work with program windows so that you can keep your desktop neat and your programs easier to find.

For example, you can minimize a window to clear it from the desktop, and you can maximize a window to give yourself more room to work within the window. Similarly, you can also move a window so that it does not overlap something else you want to see on the screen, and you can resize windows so that they do not overlap each other.

Work with Program Windows

MINIMIZE A WINDOW

① Click the **Minimize** button (▢).

● The window disappears from the screen, but its taskbar button remains visible.

MAXIMIZE A WINDOW

① Click the **Maximize**
button (☐).

● The window enlarges to fill the
entire desktop.

Note: *You can also maximize a
window by double-clicking its
title bar.*

Note: *Another way to maximize
a window is to drag its title bar
to the top of the screen. When
you release the mouse button,
Windows 7 maximizes the
window.*

**Is there a faster way to minimize all my
open windows?**
To see your desktop without minimizing,
position the mouse � over the **Show desktop**
bar on the right edge of the taskbar. To
minimize all your open windows, click the
Show desktop bar, or right-click the taskbar
and then click **Show the desktop**.

**Is it possible to maximize a
minimized window?**
Yes. To do this, press and hold
the Shift key and then right-
click the window's taskbar
button. In the menu that
appears, click **Maximize**.

continued

Work with Program Windows *(continued)*

Are you ready for more window techniques? Windows 7 uses many windows, so the more you know, the faster and more efficiently you can work.

For example, you should know how to *restore* a window. This means that you return the window to its original size and location after you have either minimized it or maximized it. You also need to know how to close a window that you no longer need and reduce clutter on the desktop.

Work with Program Windows *(continued)*

RESTORE A WINDOW

1️⃣ If the window is maximized, click the **Restore** button (🔲).

If the window is minimized, click its taskbar button instead.

● The window returns to its previous size and location.

CLOSE A WINDOW

1 Click the **Close** button (X).

The window disappears from the screen.

● If the window has a taskbar button, the button disappears from the taskbar.

Note: *If the window contains a document, the program may ask if you want to save any changes you made in the document before closing.*

Simplify It

Can I work with program windows via the keyboard?
Yes, you do this by using the *system menu* that comes with each window. Press
Alt + Spacebar or click the system menu icon in the upper left corner to display
the menu, press ↑ and ↓ on the keyboard to highlight the command you
want, and then press Enter. If you choose **Move** or **Size** from the system menu,
use the keyboard ↑, ↓, ←, and → to move or size the window, and then press
Enter. Also, you can usually press Ctrl + F4 to close a program window.

continued

33

Work with Program Windows *(continued)*

If you have information on the desktop or in a window that you want to see, but another window is covering some or all of that information, you can move the other window out of the way.

If after moving the window you find that it still covers up part of the screen item, you can also resize the window.

Similarly, if your windows overlap each other, making it hard to read what is in other windows, you can move the windows around or resize them.

Work with Program Windows *(continued)*

CHANGE THE WINDOW SIZE

① Position the mouse ⬦ over the window border that you want to move.

● The ⬦ changes to a two-headed arrow (⇕).

Note: *If the pointer does not change, it means the window cannot be resized.*

② Click and drag the ⇕ to make the window larger or smaller.

Windows 7 moves the border along with the ⇕.

③ Release the mouse button.

● Windows 7 resizes the window.

Note: *To resize two borders at once, click and drag any corner of the window.*

MOVE A WINDOW

1 Position the mouse over an empty section of the window's title bar.

2 Click and drag the mouse in the direction you want the window to move.

Windows 7 moves the window along with the mouse.

3 Release the mouse button.

● Windows 7 moves the window.

When I have several windows open, is there an easier way to size them so that none of the windows overlap?
Use Windows 7's Side by Side feature: Right-click an empty section of the taskbar and then click **Show windows side by side**. Windows 7 divides the desktop to give each window an equal amount of space.

When I have several windows open, is there an easier way to move them so that the windows are arranged neatly?
Use Windows 7's Stack feature: Right-click an empty section of the taskbar and then click **Show windows stacked**. Windows 7 arranges the windows in a tidy diagonal pattern from the top left corner of the desktop.

Using Scrollbars

If the entire content of a document is too long to fit inside a window, you can see the rest of the document by using the window's vertical scrollbar to move the content up and down.

In some scenarios the content may be too wide to fit inside a window. In such cases, you can see the rest of the document by using the window's horizontal scrollbar to move the content left and right.

Scrollbars also appear in many list boxes, so knowing how to work with scrollbars also helps you use dialog boxes.

SCROLL UP OR DOWN IN A WINDOW

1 Click and drag the vertical scroll box down or up to scroll through a window.

You can also click the up arrow (⬆) or down arrow (⬇).

● The text scrolls down or up.

SCROLL RIGHT OR LEFT IN A WINDOW

① Click and drag the horizontal scroll box.

You can also click the right arrow (▷) or the left arrow (◁).

● The text scrolls left or right.

Simplify It

What is the wheel on my mouse used for?
Not everyone's mouse has a wheel, but if yours does, you can use the wheel for scrolling up or down in a document. It works the same way as clicking the up arrow (▲) or the down arrow (▼) does. Move the wheel backward, toward your arm, and the document scrolls down; move the wheel forward, toward your computer, and the document scrolls up.

Switch Between Programs

With Windows 7, you can run two or more programs at the same time, a technique called *multitasking*. For example, you could have your word processor, your e-mail program, and your Web browser running at the same time.

However many programs you are currently multitasking, you need to know how to switch from one to another.

You can switch from one program to another using either the taskbar or the keyboard.

Switch Between Programs

SWITCH PROGRAMS USING THE TASKBAR

① Click the taskbar button of the program to which you want to switch.

Note: *A program does not have to be minimized to the taskbar for you to use the program's taskbar button.*

● Windows 7 brings the program's window to the foreground.

Note: *You can also switch to another window by clicking the window, even if it is the background.*

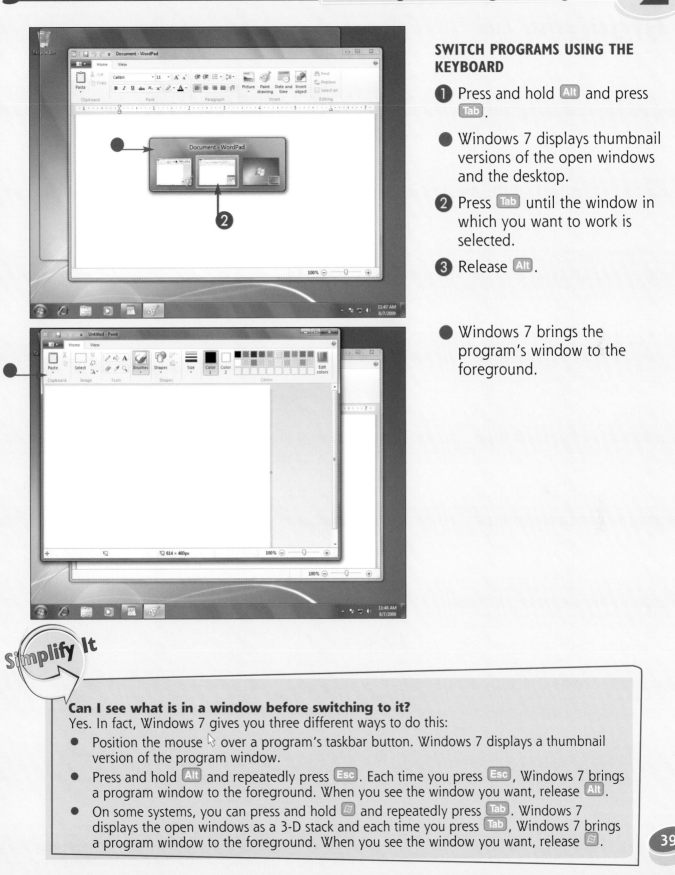

SWITCH PROGRAMS USING THE KEYBOARD

1 Press and hold `Alt` and press `Tab`.

● Windows 7 displays thumbnail versions of the open windows and the desktop.

2 Press `Tab` until the window in which you want to work is selected.

3 Release `Alt`.

● Windows 7 brings the program's window to the foreground.

Simplify It

Can I see what is in a window before switching to it?
Yes. In fact, Windows 7 gives you three different ways to do this:

● Position the mouse ⇖ over a program's taskbar button. Windows 7 displays a thumbnail version of the program window.

● Press and hold `Alt` and repeatedly press `Esc`. Each time you press `Esc`, Windows 7 brings a program window to the foreground. When you see the window you want, release `Alt`.

● On some systems, you can press and hold ⊞ and repeatedly press `Tab`. Windows 7 displays the open windows as a 3-D stack and each time you press `Tab`, Windows 7 brings a program window to the foreground. When you see the window you want, release ⊞.

Take Advantage of Program Jump Lists

You can use the new jump list feature in Windows 7 to open files or run program tasks. A *jump list* is a list associated with each program that supports this feature. Most jump lists consist of items you most recently used in the program, but some jump lists also include common program tasks.

The recent items you see on a program's jump list are called *destinations*, and they can be files, folders, Web sites, or whatever type of data the program supports.

Take Advantage of Program Jump Lists

OPEN A DESTINATION

1 Right-click the program's taskbar icon.

2 Click the destination.

Windows 7 launches the program if it is not already running and opens the destination.

RUN A TASK

1 Right-click the program's taskbar icon.

2 Click the task.

Windows 7 launches the program if it is not already running and runs the task.

Simplify It

Is there a way to ensure that a particular destination always appears on a program's jump list?
Yes, you can *pin* the destination to the jump list, which means an icon for the destination always appears in the Pinned section of the jump list. If the destination is already on the jump list, right-click the destination and then click **Pin to this list**. Otherwise, locate the file in Windows Explorer, click and drag the file and then drop it on the program's taskbar icon.

Can I remove a destination from a jump list?
Yes. Right-click the program's taskbar icon to display the jump list. Right-click the destination you want to remove and then click **Remove from this list**. If you pinned a destination as described in the previous tip, you can remove the destination from the pinned area. Right-click the pinned destination and then click **Unpin from this list**.

Uninstall a Program

When you plan to no longer use a program, you should uninstall it from your computer. Uninstalling a program means that you delete all of the program's files from your computer, and remove the program's icons from the Start menu, desktop, and taskbar. Fortunately, either the program itself or Windows 7 takes care of all these uninstall details automatically, so you only need to start the process.

Removing unused programs frees up disk space and makes your All Programs menu easier to navigate.

Uninstall a Program

① Click **Start**.

② Click **Control Panel**.

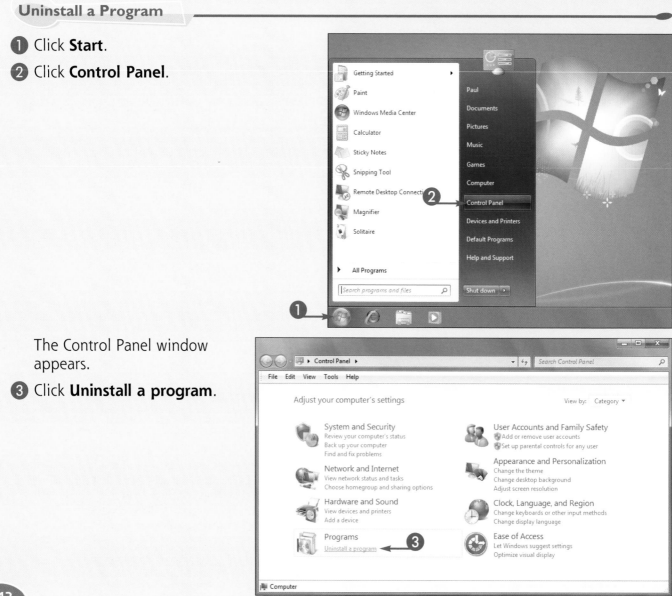

The Control Panel window appears.

③ Click **Uninstall a program**.

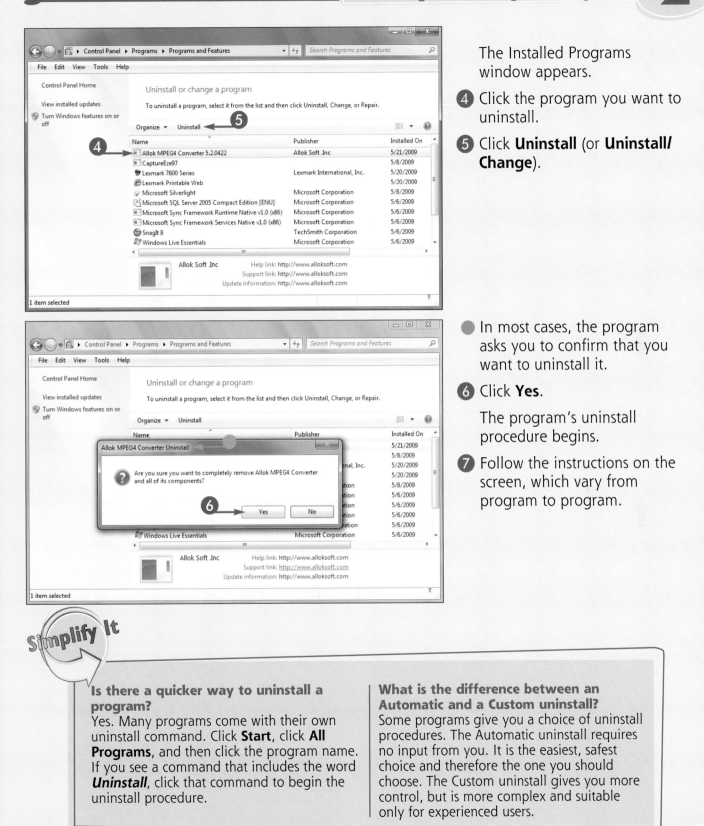

The Installed Programs window appears.

4 Click the program you want to uninstall.

5 Click **Uninstall** (or **Uninstall/ Change**).

● In most cases, the program asks you to confirm that you want to uninstall it.

6 Click **Yes**.

The program's uninstall procedure begins.

7 Follow the instructions on the screen, which vary from program to program.

Simplify It

Is there a quicker way to uninstall a program?
Yes. Many programs come with their own uninstall command. Click **Start**, click **All Programs**, and then click the program name. If you see a command that includes the word **Uninstall**, click that command to begin the uninstall procedure.

What is the difference between an Automatic and a Custom uninstall?
Some programs give you a choice of uninstall procedures. The Automatic uninstall requires no input from you. It is the easiest, safest choice and therefore the one you should choose. The Custom uninstall gives you more control, but is more complex and suitable only for experienced users.

Chapter 3

Creating and Editing Documents

To get productive with Windows 7, you need to know how to work with documents. In this chapter, you begin by learning what documents are and what types of documents you can create. From there, you learn how to create your own documents and how to save your work. You also get the details on opening documents and you learn the basic editing techniques, such as deleting characters, selecting text, and copying and moving text. You also learn how to change the font, find and replace text, and print documents.

Understanding Documents

Although your computer comes with thousands of files, only a few of them can be considered documents. That is because a document is a file that you either create yourself, or that you can open and edit yourself.

Most documents consist of text, but you can also create documents that are pictures. The four examples shown here are the basic document types that you can create using the programs that come with Windows 7.

Text Document

A text document is one that includes only the characters that you see on your keyboard, plus a few others. A text document contains no special formatting, such as colored text or bold formatting, although you can change the font. In Windows 7 you normally use the Notepad program to create text documents (although you can also use WordPad).

```
To-Do List - Notepad
File  Edit  Format  View  Help
To-Do List
=================================
-Call to arrange train tickets
-Phone Karen re: Dinner tonight
-Reschedule client meeting
-wash and vacuum car
-Set up vacation stop for newspaper
-Send deposit check for cottage rental
```

Word Processing Document

A word processing document contains text and other symbols, but you can format those characters to improve the look of the document. For example, you can change the size, color, and typeface, and you can make words bold or italic. In Windows 7, you use the WordPad program to create word processing — or Rich Text Format — documents.

Drawing

A drawing in this context is a digital image you create using special "tools" that create lines, boxes, polygons, special effects, and free-form shapes. In Windows 7, you use the Paint program to create drawings.

E-mail Message

An e-mail message is a document that you send to another person via the Internet. Most e-mail messages use plain text, but some programs support formatted text, images, and other effects. In Windows 7, you can download and install the Windows Live Mail program to create and send e-mail messages (see Chapter 9).

Create a Document

When you are ready to create something using Windows 7, in most cases you begin by opening the appropriate program — such as Windows Live Mail if you want to create an e-mail message — and then using the program to create a new document to hold your work.

Many Windows 7 programs (such as WordPad and Paint) create a new document for you automatically when you begin the program. However, you can also create another new document any time you need one.

Create a Document

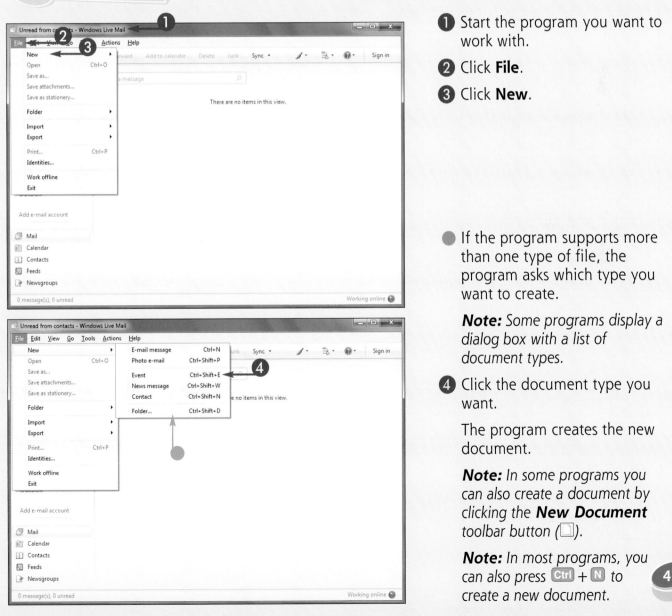

① Start the program you want to work with.

② Click **File**.

③ Click **New**.

● If the program supports more than one type of file, the program asks which type you want to create.

Note: *Some programs display a dialog box with a list of document types.*

④ Click the document type you want.

The program creates the new document.

Note: *In some programs you can also create a document by clicking the **New Document** toolbar button ( ).*

Note: *In most programs, you can also press* Ctrl + N *to create a new document.*

Save a Document

After you create a document and make any changes to it, you can save the document to preserve your work.

Saving your work is important because when you work on a document, Windows 7 stores the changes in your computer's memory, which is erased each time you shut down or restart your computer. When you save a document, Windows 7 stores your changes on your computer's hard drive. Because the contents of the hard drive are preserved when you shut down or restart your computer, you do not lose your work.

Save a Document

1 Click **File** (▣).

2 Click **Save**.

Note: In most programs, you can also press Ctrl + S or click the **Save** button (▣).

Note: If you saved the document previously, your changes are now preserved. You do not need to follow the rest of the steps in this section.

If this is a new document that you have never saved before, the Save As dialog box appears.

3 Click here to see a list of your folders.

4 Click **Documents**.

Note: In most programs, the Documents folder is selected automatically when you save a document.

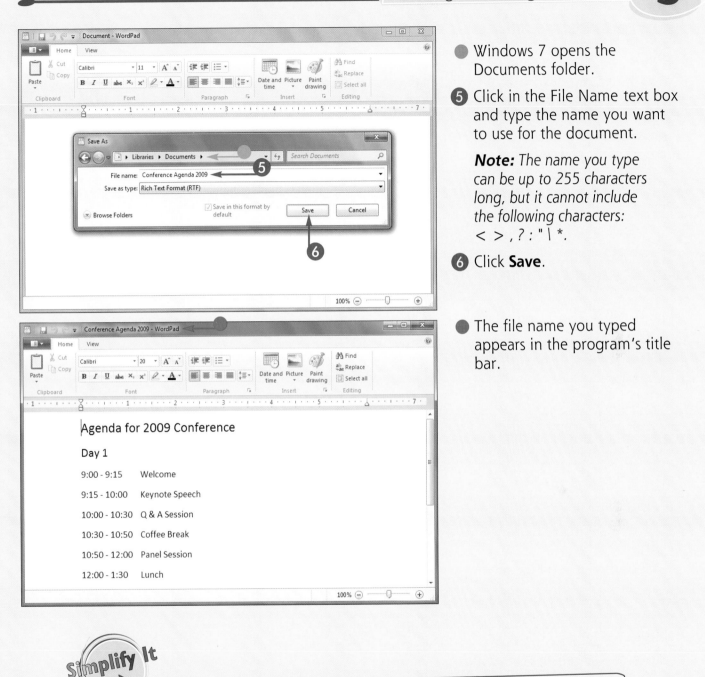

● Windows 7 opens the Documents folder.

⑤ Click in the File Name text box and type the name you want to use for the document.

Note: *The name you type can be up to 255 characters long, but it cannot include the following characters:* < > , ? : " \ *.

⑥ Click **Save**.

● The file name you typed appears in the program's title bar.

Can I create different types of documents in a program?
Yes, in most programs. With WordPad, for example, you can create both word processing documents and text documents. However, a program such as Notepad supports only text documents. If the program supports multiple document types, the Save As dialog box includes a drop-down list named Save As Type (or something similar). Use that list to choose the document type you want.

Open a Document

To work with a document that you have saved in the past, you need to open the document in the program that you used to create it.

When you save a document, Windows 7 stores the document contents in a file on your hard drive. Opening the document means that

Windows 7 locates the file on the hard drive and then loads its contents into your computer's memory. This enables you to read, edit, and add to the document using the original program.

Open a Document

1 Start the program you want to work with.

2 Click **File** (▣).

Note: *If you see the document you want in a list of the most recently used documents on the File menu, click the name to open it. You can skip the rest of the steps in this section.*

3 Click **Open**.

Note: *In most programs, you can also press* Ctrl *+* O *or click the* ***Open*** *button (▣).*

The Open dialog box appears.

4 Double-click **Documents**.

Note: *In most programs, the Documents folder is selected automatically when you open a document.*

● If you want to open the document from some other folder, click here, click your user name, and then double-click the folder.

● Windows 7 opens the Documents folder.

⑤ Click the document name.

⑥ Click **Open**.

● The document appears in the program window.

Is there a more direct way to open a document?
Yes there is. You do not always need to open the program first. Instead, open the folder that contains the document and then double-click the document. Windows 7 automatically launches the program and opens the document.

① Click **Start**.

② Click **Documents**.

The Documents library appears.

③ Double-click the document.

Windows 7 starts the program in which you created the document and then opens the document.

Edit Document Text

When you work with a character-based file, such as a text document, a word processing document, or an e-mail message, you need to know the basic techniques for editing the document text.

The most fundamental editing technique involves deleting existing characters that you no longer need or that you typed accidentally or in error. However, you also need to know how to select text, which then enables you to copy or move that text.

Edit Document Text

DELETE CHARACTERS

① Click immediately to the left of the first character you want to delete.

● The cursor appears before the character.

② Press **Delete** until you have deleted all the characters you want.

Note: *An alternative method is to click immediately to the right of the last character you want to delete and then press* **Backspace** *until you have deleted all the characters you want.*

Note: *If you make a mistake, immediately press* **Ctrl** + **Z** *or click the* **Undo** *button (⤺). Alternatively, click* **Edit**, *and then click* **Undo**.

SELECT TEXT FOR EDITING

1 Click and drag across the text you want to select.

2 Release the mouse button.

● The program highlights the selected text.

Agenda for 2010 Conference

Day 1

9:00 - 9:15   Welcome

9:15 - 10:00   Keynote Speech

10:00 - 10:30   Q & A Session

10:30 - 10:50   Coffee Break

10:50 - 12:00   Panel Session

<div class="simplify-it">

Simplify It

Are there any shortcut methods I can use to select text in WordPad?
Yes. Here are the most useful ones:

- Click in the white space to the left of a line to select the line.
- Double-click a word to select it.
- Triple-click inside a paragraph to select it.
- Press **Ctrl** + **A** to select the entire document.
- For a long selection, click to the left of the first character you want to select, scroll to the end of the selection using the scroll bar, press and hold **Shift**, and then click to the right of the last character you want to select.

</div>

continued

Edit Document Text *(continued)*

Once you select some text, the program treats the selection as though it was a single object. This means that you can work with all of the selected characters together, which is much faster than working with one character at a time.

For example, if you need to delete a large section of text, it is much faster to select the text first and then delete it all at once.

Similarly, you can also select your text and then apply a text font, as described in the "Change the Text Font" section.

You can also copy or move selected text to a different location within the document, as described in the rest of this section.

Edit Document Text *(continued)*

COPY TEXT

① Select the text you want to copy.

② Click **Copy** (🗐).

Note: *In most programs, you can also press* Ctrl + C *or click the **Edit** menu and then click **Copy**.*

③ Click inside the document at the position where you want the copy of the text to appear.

The cursor appears in the position you clicked.

④ Click **Paste** (🗐).

Note: *In most programs, you can also press* Ctrl + V *or click the **Edit** menu and then click **Paste**.*

● The program inserts a copy of the selected text at the cursor position.

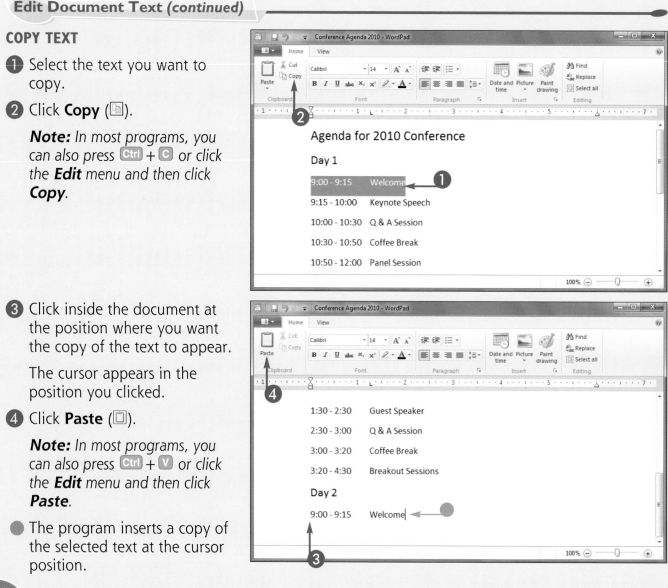

Day 2

9:00 - 9:15	Welcome
9:15 - 10:00	President's Speech
11:00 - 12:00	2010 Forecast
10:00 - 10:40	2009 Recap
10:40 - 11:00	Coffee Break

Day 2

9:00 - 9:15	Welcome
9:15 - 10:00	President's Speech
10:00 - 10:40	2009 Recap
10:40 - 11:00	Coffee Break
11:00 - 12:00	2010 Forecast

MOVE TEXT

1 Select the text you want to move.

2 Click **Cut** (✂).

Note: *In most programs, you can also press* Ctrl *+* X *or click the* **Edit** *menu and then click* **Cut**.

The program removes the text from the document.

3 Click inside the document at the position where you want to move the text.

The cursor appears at the position you clicked.

4 Click **Paste** (📋).

Note: *In most programs, you can also press* Ctrl *+* V *or click the* **Edit** *menu and then click* **Paste**.

● The program inserts the text at the cursor position.

Simplify It

How do I move and copy text with my mouse?
First, select the text you want to work with. To move the selected text, position the mouse ⬚ over the selection, and then click and drag the text to the new position within the document.

To copy the selected text, position the mouse ⬚ over the selection, press and hold Ctrl, and then click and drag the text to the desired position within the document.

Change the Text Font

When you work in a word processing document, you can add visual appeal by changing the font formatting of some or all of the text.

The font formatting determines how the characters appear in the document. For example, one common font attribute is the typeface, which determines the overall look of each character. You can also change the font style — which determines whether the text appears as bold or italic — and the font size. Most programs also offer several font special effects, such as underline or colors.

Change the Text Font

① Select the text you want to format.

② Display the font options.

● In WordPad, you display the font options by clicking the **Home** tab.

Note: In many other programs, you display the font options by clicking Format in the menu bar and then clicking the Font command.

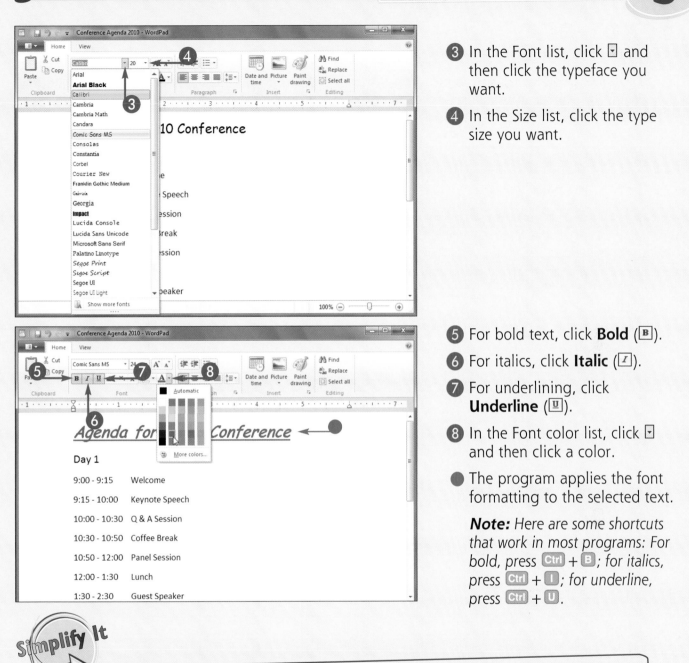

③ In the Font list, click ⊡ and then click the typeface you want.

④ In the Size list, click the type size you want.

⑤ For bold text, click **Bold** (B).

⑥ For italics, click **Italic** (I).

⑦ For underlining, click **Underline** (U).

⑧ In the Font color list, click ⊡ and then click a color.

● The program applies the font formatting to the selected text.

Note: *Here are some shortcuts that work in most programs: For bold, press* Ctrl *+* B *; for italics, press* Ctrl *+* I *; for underline, press* Ctrl *+* U *.*

Simplify It

How can I make the best use of fonts in my documents?

● Do not use many different typefaces in a single document. Stick to one or at most two typefaces to avoid the "ransom note look."

● Avoid overly decorative typefaces because they are often difficult to read.

● Use bold only for document titles, subtitles, and headings.

● Use italics only to emphasize words and phrases, or for the titles of books and magazines.

● Use larger type sizes only for document titles, subtitles, and, possibly, the headings.

● If you change the text color, be sure to leave enough contrast between the text and the background. In general, dark text on a light background is the easiest to read.

Find Text

In large documents, when you need to find a specific word or phrase, you can save a lot of time by using the program's Find feature, which searches the entire document in the blink of an eye.

Most programs that work with text — including Windows 7's WordPad and Notepad programs — have the Find feature. You can also work with the Find feature in programs such as Internet Explorer and Windows Live Mail.

Find Text

① Click **Find** (⚟).

> **Note:** In many programs, you run the Find command by clicking **Edit** in the menu bar and then clicking the **Find** command, or by pressing Ctrl + F.

The Find dialog box appears.

② Click in the Find What text box and type the text you want to find.

③ Click **Find Next**.

to a room with various cultural and sociological artifacts. The Czech playwright

Daniela Fischerova said it best: "Every new word is a new reality."

New word that coin the

also our way things are even

as they al ooal mine), giving us a

glimpse of (or a warning about) what's to come. Here's the lexicographer Victoria

Neufeldt on this neologism-as-cultural-reflection idea:

The *neologisms* that especially capture our attention are indeed often

remarkable; some with their metaphorical baggage can constitute

Find

Find what: neologisms   [Find Next]

☐ Match whole word only   [Cancel]

☐ Match case

coinages into cocktail party conversations).

I came down with this affliction many years ago, and I've been clam-happy ever

since. I enjoy words and language in general, but what sets my crank a-turning is, as

H. L. Mencken said, "the biology of language, as opposed to its paleontology." I love

the *living language* more than the fossilized variety with its hardened meanings and

set-in-stone lexicon. To put it another way, although I get as much pleasure as

anyone out of a dictionary, the words it contains are, well, domesticated. I love the

untamed neologisms that romp around the linguistic wilderness. When I see a

new word in an article or book, I get a little jolt of excitement, a mental shock akin to

● The program selects the next instance of the search text.

Note: If the search text does not exist in the document, the program usually displays a dialog box to let you know.

④ If the selected instance is not the one you want, click **Find Next** until the program finds the correct instance.

⑤ Click the **Close** button (☒) to close the Find dialog box.

● The program leaves the found text selected.

Simplify It

When I search for a small word such as the, the program matches it in larger words such as theme and bother. How can I avoid this?
In the Find dialog box, click **Match whole word only** (☐ changes to ☑). This tells the program to match the search text only if it is a word on its own and not part of another word.

When I search for a name such as Bill, the program also matches the non-name bill. Is there a way to fix this?
In the Find dialog box, click **Match case** (☐ changes to ☑). This tells the program to match the search text only if it has the same mix of uppercase and lowercase letters that you specify in the Find What text box. If you type **Bill**, for example, the program matches only *Bill* and not *bill*.

Replace Text

Do you need to replace a word or part of a word with some other text? Normally you would open the document and then edit the text directly. However, if you have several instances to replace, you can save time and do a more accurate job if you let the program's Replace feature make the changes for you.

Most programs that work with text — including Windows 7's WordPad and Notepad programs — have the Replace feature.

Replace Text

1 Click **Replace** (⬚).

> **Note:** In many programs, you run the Find command by clicking **Edit** in the menu bar and then clicking the **Replace** command, or by pressing **Ctrl** + **H**.

The Replace dialog box appears.

2 In the Find What text box, enter the text you want to find.

3 Click in the Replace With text box and type the text you want to use as the replacement.

4 Click **Find Next**.

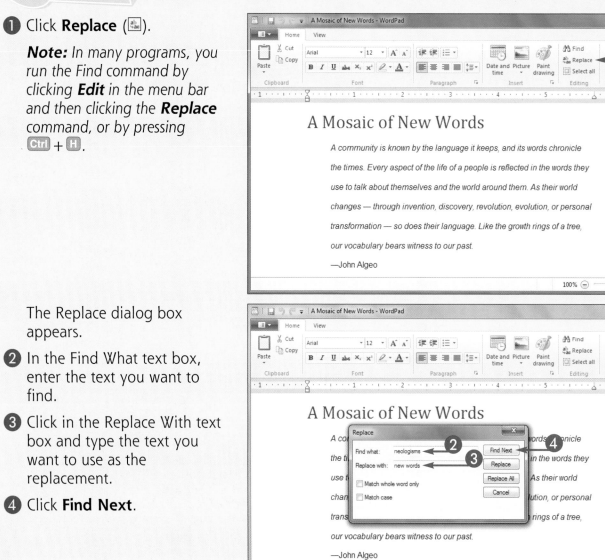

The program selects the next instance of the search text.

Note: *If the search text does not exist in the document, the program displays a dialog box to let you know.*

5 If the selected instance is not the one you want, click **Find Next** until the program finds the correct instance.

6 Click **Replace**.

The program replaces the selected text with the replacement text.

The program selects the next instance of the search text.

7 Repeat Steps **5** and **6** until you have replaced all of the instances you want to replace.

8 Click the **Close** button (☒) to close the Replace dialog box.

Simplify It

Is there a faster way to replace every instance of the search text with the replacement text?
Yes. In the Replace dialog box, click **Replace All**. This tells the program to replace every instance of the search text with the replacement text. However, you should exercise some caution with this feature because it may make some replacements that you did not intend. Click **Find Next** a few times to make sure the matches are correct. Also, consider clicking the **Match whole word only** and **Match case** check boxes (☐ changes to ☑), as described in the "Find Text" section in this chapter.

Print a Document

When you need a hard copy of your document, either for your files or to distribute to someone else, you can get a paper copy by sending the document to your printer. If you happen to have more than one printer, you can specify which device you prefer to use for the document.

All programs enable you to specify in advance how many copies you want to print. In most cases you can also tell the program to print only part of the document, if that is all you need.

Print a Document

① Turn on your printer.

② Open the document you want to print.

③ Click **File** (▣).

④ Click **Print**.

> **Note:** In many programs, you can select the **Print** command by pressing Ctrl + P or by clicking the **Print** button (⬚).

The Print dialog box appears.

Note: The layout of the Print dialog box varies from program to program. The WordPad version shown here is a typical example.

⑤ If you have more than one printer, click the printer you want to use.

⑥ Use the **Number of copies** ⬍ to specify the number of copies to print.

⑦ Click **Print**.

● Windows 7 prints the document. The print icon (🖶) appears in the taskbar's notification area while the document prints.

Simplify It

How do I print only part of a document?
Most programs enable you to use the following methods to print only part of the document:

- Print selected text: Select the text you want to print. In the Print dialog box, click **Selection** (◯ changes to ◉).

- Print a specific page: Place the cursor on the page you want to print. In the Print dialog box, click **Current Page** (◯ changes to ◉).

- Print a range of pages: In the Print dialog box, click **Pages** (◯ changes to ◉). In the text box, type the first page number, a dash (–), and the last page number (for example, 1–5).

Chapter 4

Working with Images

Whether you load your images from a device, download them from the Internet, or draw them yourself, Windows 7 comes with a number of useful tools for working with those images. For example, you can use the Pictures library to see a preview of an image and to open an image for viewing. You can also use Windows 7 to scan a photo or other image from a scanner, and you can import photos that you have taken with a digital camera. You can also make repairs to an image and print hard copies of your photos.

Open the Pictures Library

Before you can work with your images, you need to view them on your computer. You do that by opening Windows 7's Pictures library, which is a special folder designed specifically for storing images.

As you see later in this chapter, you can use the Pictures library to preview an image and open an image file. Also, when you import an image using a scanner or digital camera, Windows 7 usually stores the resulting files in the Pictures library.

Open the Pictures Library

1 Click **Start**.

2 Click **Pictures**.

The Pictures library appears.

Preview an Image

You can preview any saved image file using either the Details pane or the Preview pane in the Pictures library. The Details pane, located at the bottom of the window, also displays details about the file, such as the file type, dimensions, and size. The Preview pane, which appears on the right side of the window, shows a larger preview of the image.

You can also use the Preview pane to preview images stored in *subfolders* — folders stored within the main Pictures library.

Preview an Image

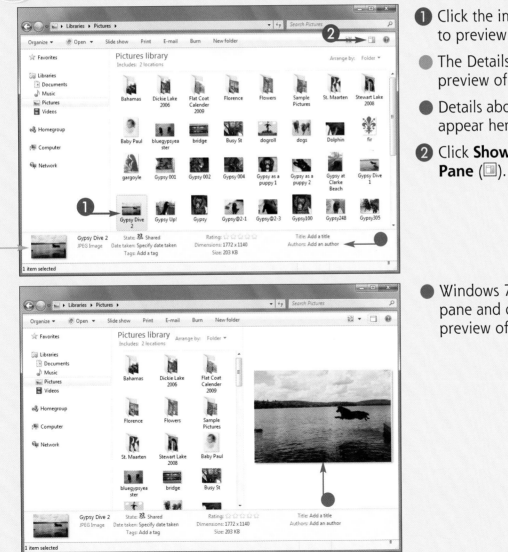

1 Click the image file you want to preview.

● The Details pane shows a small preview of the image.

● Details about the image file appear here.

2 Click **Show the Preview Pane** (▣).

● Windows 7 opens the Preview pane and displays a larger preview of the image.

View Your Images

If you want to look at several images, you can use Windows Photo Viewer to navigate backwards and forwards through the images in the Pictures library.

You can also view the images in your Pictures library using Windows Live Photo Gallery, if you have that program installed on your computer.

See Chapter 9 to learn how to install Windows Live Photo Gallery.

You can also use either program to zoom in and out of an image and to run an image slide show.

View Your Images

VIEW IMAGES USING WINDOWS PHOTO VIEWER

1 Click the image.

2 Click the **Open** ⊡.

3 Click **Windows Photo Viewer**.

The image opens in Windows Photo Viewer.

4 To get a closer look at the image, click the magnifying glass and then click and drag the slider up.

5 To view the next image in the folder, click the **Next** button (▶).

6 To view the previous image in the folder, click the **Previous** button (◀).

7 To start a slide show of all the images in the folder, click the **Play Slide Show** button (▣).

Note: To stop the slide show, press Esc.

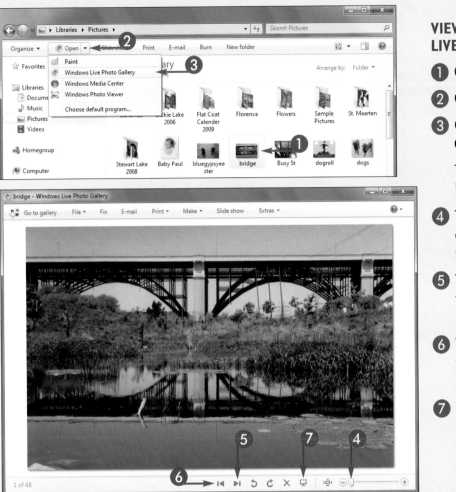

VIEW IMAGES USING WINDOWS LIVE PHOTO GALLERY

1 Click the image.

2 Click the **Open** ▾.

3 Click **Windows Live Photo Gallery**.

The image opens in Windows Live Photo Gallery.

4 To see more of the image, click and drag the slider to the right.

5 To view the next image in the folder, click the **Next** button (▷).

6 To view the previous image in the folder, click the **Previous** button (◁).

7 To start a slide show of all the images in the folder, click the **Play Slide Show** button (▢).

Note: *To stop the slide show, press* Esc.

Simplify It

Is there a way I can view my pictures without using the Photo Gallery Viewer?

Yes, you can change the Picture folder's view to display large *thumbnails* — scaled-down versions of the actual images:

1 Click the **Views** ▾.

2 Click **Extra Large Icons**.

● Windows 7 displays the images as thumbnails.

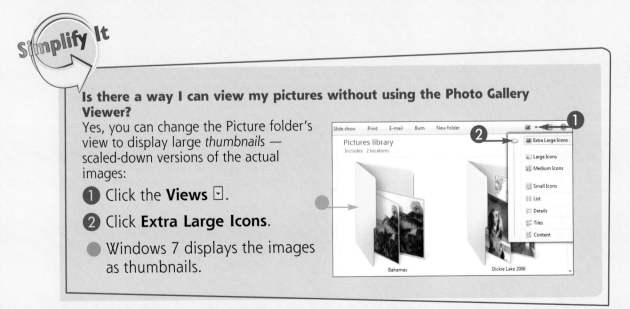

Scan an Image

You can create a digital copy of a photo or other image by using a document scanner, or the scanner component of an all-in-one printer. The scanner copies the image to your computer, where you can then store it as a file on your hard drive.

There are many ways you can use a scanned image. For example, you can scan a photo to e-mail to friends or publish on a Web page. You can also scan a logo or other image to use in a document.

Scan an Image

① Turn on your scanner or all-in-one printer and position a photo or other image on the scanner bed.

② Click **Start**.

③ Click **Devices and Printers**.

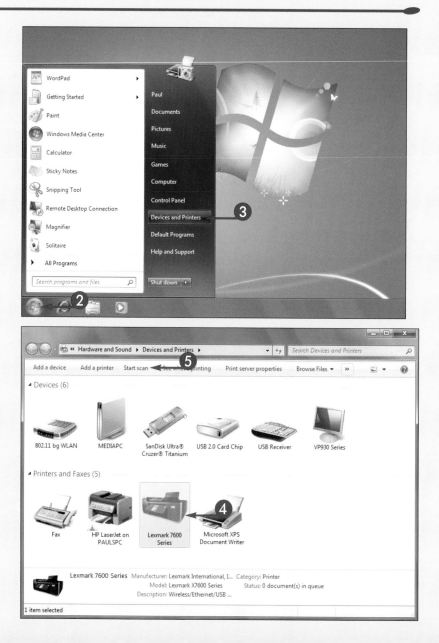

The Devices and Printers window appears.

④ Click the device you want to use to perform the scan.

⑤ Click **Start scan**.

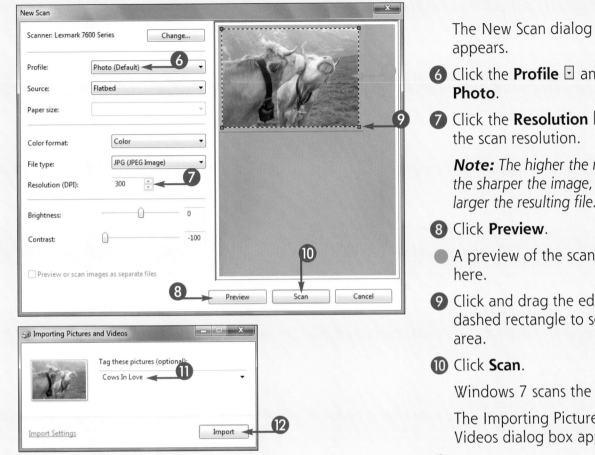

The New Scan dialog box appears.

⑥ Click the **Profile** ⊡ and then click **Photo**.

⑦ Click the **Resolution** ⊞ to specify the scan resolution.

Note: The higher the resolution, the sharper the image, but the larger the resulting file.

⑧ Click **Preview**.

● A preview of the scan appears here.

⑨ Click and drag the edges of the dashed rectangle to set the scan area.

⑩ Click **Scan**.

Windows 7 scans the image.

The Importing Pictures and Videos dialog box appears.

⑪ Type a word or phrase that describes the scan.

⑫ Click **Import**.

Windows 7 imports the image to your computer.

How do I view a picture I have previously scanned?
Windows 7 stores the image in the Pictures library. It creates a new folder, the name of which is the current date followed by whatever word or phrase you type in the Importing Pictures and Videos dialog box; for example, 2009-08-23 Flower. Open the subfolder to see your scanned picture.

Are there other methods I can use to scan an image?
Yes. Most scanners or all-in-one printers come with a Scan button that you can push to start a new scan. You can also click **Start**, **All Programs**, **Windows Fax and Scan**, and then **New Scan**. In Paint (click **Start**, **All Programs**, **Accessories**, and then **Paint**), click the **File** menu and then click **From scanner or camera**. In Windows Live Photo Gallery (click **Start**, **All Programs**, **Windows Live**, and then **Windows Live Photo Gallery**), click **File** and then click **Import from a camera or scanner**.

Import Images from a Digital Camera

If you have used your digital camera to take pictures, you can use Windows 7 to import those photos from the camera and save them on your computer. If your camera stores the photos on a memory card, you can also use a memory card reader attached to your computer to upload the digital photos from the removable drive that Windows 7 sets up.

Once you have the digital photos on your system, you can view the photos, make repairs or adjustments to the files, or print the images.

Import Images from a Digital Camera

1 Plug in your camera or memory storage card reader.

The AutoPlay dialog box appears.

2 Click **Import Pictures and Videos using Windows**.

The Import Pictures and Videos dialog box appears.

3 Type a word or phrase that describes the photos.

4 Click **Import**.

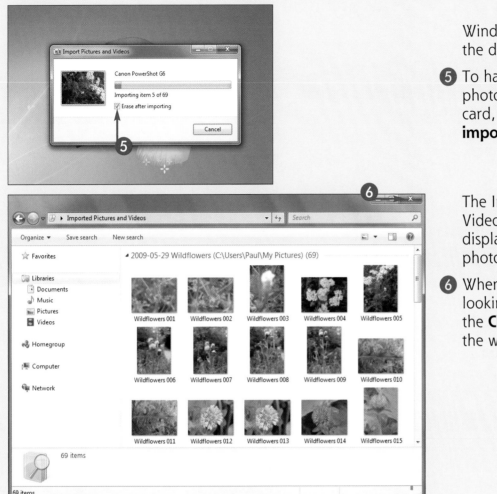

Windows 7 begins importing the digital photos.

⑤ To have Windows 7 erase the photos from the camera or card, click **Erase after importing** (☐ changes to ☑).

The Imported Pictures and Videos window appears and displays the recently imported photos.

⑥ When you have finished looking at your photos, click the **Close** button (☒) to close the window.

Simplify It

How do I view the imported photos?
If you have closed the Imported Pictures and Videos window, note that Windows 7 stores the imported digital photos in the Pictures library. It creates a new subfolder, the name of which is the current date followed by whatever word or phrase you type in the Importing Pictures and Videos dialog box. For example, if the current date is August 23, 2009 and you typed **Nassau Vacation** in the text box, the new subfolder will be named 2009-08-23 Nassau Vacation. Open the subfolder to see your imported digital photos.

Repair a Digital Image

You can use Windows Live Photo Gallery to improve the look of digital photos and other images. Windows Live Photo Gallery includes a special Fix window that offers a number of tools for repairing various image attributes.

The Fix window enables you to adjust an image's brightness, contrast, color temperature, tint, and saturation. You can also crop and rotate an image and fix red eye. Windows Live Photo Gallery also comes with a feature that can make many of these adjustments for you automatically.

See Chapter 9 to learn how to download and install Windows Live Photo Gallery.

Repair a Digital Image

1 Click **Start**.

2 Click **All Programs**.

Note: When you click **All Programs**, the command name changes to Back.

3 Click **Windows Live**.

4 Click **Windows Live Photo Gallery**.

Windows Live Photo Gallery appears.

5 Click the image you want to repair.

6 Click **Fix** to open the Fix window.

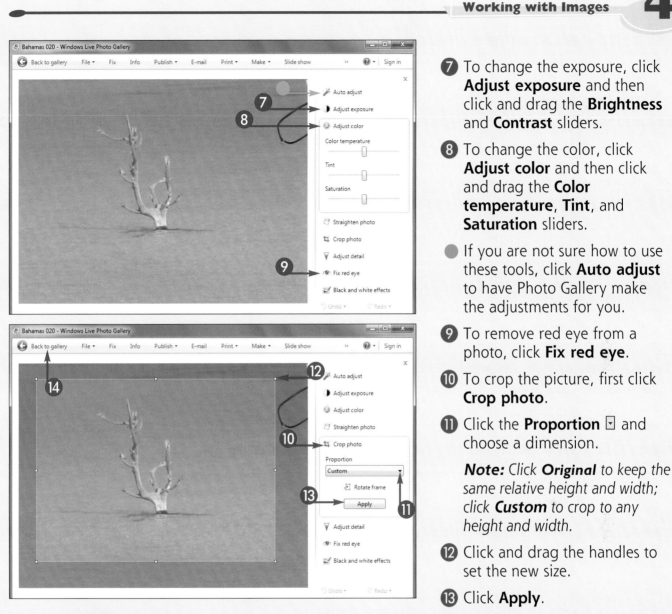

7 To change the exposure, click **Adjust exposure** and then click and drag the **Brightness** and **Contrast** sliders.

8 To change the color, click **Adjust color** and then click and drag the **Color temperature**, **Tint**, and **Saturation** sliders.

● If you are not sure how to use these tools, click **Auto adjust** to have Photo Gallery make the adjustments for you.

9 To remove red eye from a photo, click **Fix red eye**.

10 To crop the picture, first click **Crop photo**.

11 Click the **Proportion** ⊡ and choose a dimension.

Note: *Click* ***Original*** *to keep the same relative height and width; click* ***Custom*** *to crop to any height and width.*

12 Click and drag the handles to set the new size.

13 Click **Apply**.

14 When you are done, click **Back to gallery**.

Simplify It

How did my photo end up sideways?
When you take a vertical shot with your digital camera, your photo appears sideways when you download the image to your computer. You may also have scanned the image vertically instead of horizontally. In the Fix window, click ⟳ to rotate the image counterclockwise; click ↻ to rotate the image clockwise.

I do not like the repairs I made to my image. Can I get the original image back?
Yes, you can. Windows Live Photo Gallery always keeps a backup copy of the original image, just in case. To undo all your changes and get the original image back, click the image and then click **Fix**. In the Fix window, click **Revert** and then click **Revert to Original** (or press Ctrl + R).

Print
an Image

You can print an image from the Pictures library, or from any subfolder in the Pictures library. When you activate the Print task, the Print Pictures dialog box appears. You can use this dialog box to choose a printer, the paper size, the printout quality, and a layout, and to send the image to the printer.

You can print a single image or multiple images. If you work with multiple images, you can print them individually or you can select a layout that prints two or more images per sheet.

Print an Image

① In the Pictures library, select the image or images you want to print.

② Click **Print**.

The Print Pictures dialog box appears.

③ If you use more than one printer with your computer, click ⊡ and click the printer you want to use.

④ Click ⊡ and click the size of paper you are using.

⑤ Click ⊡ and click the printout quality you prefer.

Note: *Print quality is measured in dots per inch (dpi). The higher the dpi value, the better the print quality.*

⑥ Click the layout you want to use for the printed image.

● The Wizard displays a preview of the printout.

● Click the **Next** button (▣) to see previews of other pages.

⑦ Click ⊞ to select the number of copies you want.

⑧ Click **Print**.

The Wizard sends your image or images to the printer.

Simplify It

What type of paper should I use for my photo printouts?
Depending on the kind of printer you are using, you can find a variety of photo-quality paper types for printing out your digital photographs. Photo-quality paper, though more expensive than multipurpose paper, is designed to create a more permanent image and improve the resolution and color of the printed images. Photo-quality paper comes in glossy and matte finishes, as well as variations of each. Be sure to select a photo-quality paper that your printer manufacturer recommends.

Chapter 5

Playing Music and Other Media

In Windows 7, you play music and other media using the Windows Media Player program. Windows Media Player stores your music files and other media in a special library, and you can use that library to browse your music and display the files by album, artist, genre, and more.

You can also use Windows Media Player to listen to audio files stored on your computer, and to play CDs that you insert into your computer CD or DVD drive. Windows Media Player also enables you to watch video files, play DVD discs, and even create your own music CDs.

Open and Close
Windows Media Player

Windows 7 includes Windows Media Player, which is the program you will use throughout this chapter. As you learn in the next few sections, you can use Windows Media Player to navigate your media library, play back and record audio files and music CDs, adjust the

volume, as well as view video. To begin using the program, you must first learn how to open the Windows Media Player window.

When you finish using the program, you can close the Windows Media Player window to free up computer processing power.

Open and Close Windows Media Player

① Click **Windows Media Player** (![icon]) in the taskbar.

Note: *If you do not see the Media Player icon, you can also click **Start**, click **All Programs**, and then click **Windows Media Player**.*

The first time you start the program, the Welcome to Windows Media Player dialog box appears.

② Click **Recommended settings** (◎ changes to ◉).

③ Click **Finish**.

The Windows Media Player window appears.

④ When you have finished with Media Player, click the **Close** button (![X icon]) to close the window.

The Windows Media Player window closes.

Navigate the Media Player Window

The Windows Media Player interface is not complicated, but it does pay to familiarize yourself with the various elements of the Windows Media Player window. This is useful because it helps you get more out of Windows

Media Player and it ensures that you can easily navigate and activate elements when you are ready to play audio files or view videos and DVDs.

Address Bar

This area shows your current location in the Media Player library.

Tabs

The tabs are links to the key features of Windows Media Player.

Toolbar

You can use the Media Player toolbar to access commands, change the view, and search for media.

Details Pane

This pane displays information about the contents of the current library location, such as the album art and title, and the title and length of the song or video.

Playback Controls

These buttons control how a video or music file plays, and enable you to make adjustments to the sound.

Navigation Pane

You use this pane to navigate the Media Player library's categories.

Using the Library

You can use the library feature in Windows Media Player to manage all of the media files on your computer, including audio files and videos. The library also enables you to organize other digital content, such as music CDs.

When you first start using Windows Media Player, the program automatically updates the library with the files already in your computer's media folders, such as Music and Videos.

Using the Library

NAVIGATE THE LIBRARY

❶ In the Navigation pane, click the category you want to use.

❷ If the category includes subcategories, click a subcategory to see its contents.

❸ Double-click the item you want to use.

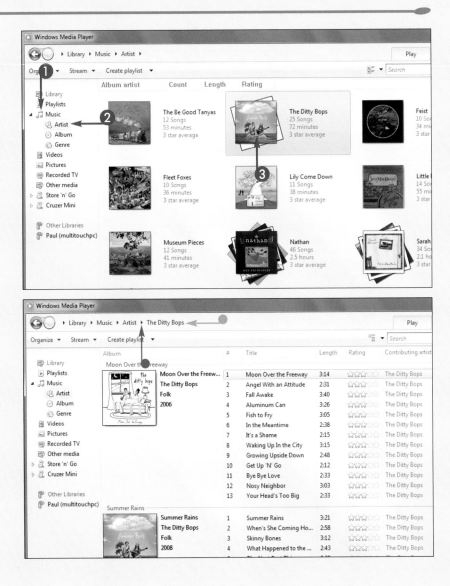

Media Player displays the contents of the item in the details pane.

● You can also click the items in the Address bar to return to a category or subcategory.

● Click an arrow to see the contents of any Address bar item.

CHANGE THE LIBRARY VIEW

1 Click the **View options** ▾.

2 Click the view you want to use.

Media Player changes the view.

My library is quite large. How do I search for a specific file?
If you want to search the entire library, click **Library** in the Address bar. Otherwise, click the category you want to search, such as **Music**. Click in the search box on the right side of the toolbar. Type a word or phrase that represents the media you want to find. The matching media appear in the library.

How does the library create its folders and subfolders?
The library automatically groups music into the categories based on their media content information. Media content information, also called *metadata* or *tags*, includes information such as the artist name, song title, rating, play count, and composer. Media content information also identifies the file type.

Play an Audio or a Video File

Windows Media Player uses the library to play audio or video files that you store on your computer. When you select an audio file from a library folder and play it in Windows Media Player, you can also switch to the Now Playing window to see a visualization along with the song. You can also use the Now Playing window to control the playback of the audio or video.

When you want to choose a different song or video, you can switch back to the Windows Media Player library.

Play an Audio or a Video File

① Use the library to navigate to the folder that contains the audio or video file that you want to play.

Note: See *"Using the Library"* to learn more about working with the library's folder.

② Click the audio or video file.

③ Click the **Play** button (▶).

④ Click **Switch to Now Playing** (⊞) to view the album art while an audio file plays.

Windows Media Player begins playing the audio or video file.

⑤ Move the mouse ⊳ into the Now Playing window.

● The playback buttons appear, which enable you to control how the song or video plays.

Note: See *"Play a Music CD"* to learn more about the playback buttons.

● You can click **Switch to Library** (⊞) to return to the Media Player library.

Adjust the Volume

While an audio or video file is playing, you can adjust the playback volume up or down to get the audio just right. You can adjust the playback volume whether you are playing the

audio or video using the Windows Media Player library or the Now Playing window.

If you need to silence the audio or video temporarily, you can mute the playback.

Adjust the Volume

ADJUST THE VOLUME USING THE LIBRARY

1 Click and drag the **Volume** slider left (to reduce the volume) or right (to increase the volume).

● If you want to silence the playback, click the **Mute** button (⊡).

Note: To restore the volume, click the **Sound** button (⊡).

ADJUST THE VOLUME IN THE NOW PLAYING WINDOW

1 Move the mouse ⌖ within the Now Playing window.

The playback controls appear.

2 Click here and then drag the **Volume** slider left (to reduce the volume) or right (to increase the volume).

● To silence the playback, click the **Mute** button (⊡).

Note: To restore the volume, click the **Sound** button (⊡).

Play a Music CD

You can play your favorite music CDs in Windows Media Player. You can control some playback options using the Now Playing window, but you can also switch to the Media Player library for more options. These options include skipping a track and pausing and resuming the playback.

To play a music CD with Windows Media Player, your computer must have a CD or DVD drive.

PLAY A CD

① Insert a music CD into your computer's CD or DVD drive.

If Media Player is not already running, the Now Playing window appears and the CD begins playing.

● On commercial CDs, the album cover appears here.

② Move the mouse ⌖ within the Now Playing window.

● The playback controls appear.

SKIP A TRACK

③ Click the **Next** button (▶▶|) to skip to the next track.

④ Click the **Previous** button (|◀◀) to skip to the previous track.

PAUSE AND RESUME PLAY

⑤ Click the **Pause** button (❙❙).

Windows Media Player pauses playback.

⑥ Click the **Play** button (▶).

Windows Media Player resumes playback where you left off.

Simplify It

Can I change the CD's audio levels?
Yes, Windows Media Player has a graphic equalizer component you can work with. To display it, right-click the **Now Playing** window, click **Enhancements**, and then click **Graphic Equalizer**. To choose a predefined set of levels, click **Default**, and then click a preset value such as Rock or Classical. Alternatively, use the sliders to set your own audio levels.

Can I display something other than album art during playback?
Yes. Right-click the **Now Playing** window and then click **Visualizations** to see a list of visualization categories. Click a category and then click the visualization you want to view. The visualizations in the Battery category are fun to play with, as their names suggest: Dance of the Freaky Circles, Green Is Not Your Enemy, Spider's Last Moment, and My Tornado Is Resting.

Play a Music CD *(continued)*

You can use the playback buttons at the bottom of the Windows Media Player library to control how a CD plays. For example, you can stop the CD playback, or you can select another song to play. Windows Media Player also gives you the option to repeat the entire CD, and you can also choose to play the songs randomly.

Play a Music CD *(continued)*

STOP PLAY

⑦ Click the **Stop** button (■).

Windows Media Player stops playback.

If you click the **Play** button (▶) after clicking the **Stop** button (■), the current song starts over again.

⑧ Click **Switch to Library** (▦) to open the Media Player library window.

PLAY ANOTHER SONG

⑨ In the Details pane, double-click the song you want to play.

Windows Media Player begins playing the song.

● This area displays the current song title, the album title, and the song composer.

REPEAT THE CD

⑩ Click the **Turn Repeat On** button (⟳).

Windows Media Player restarts the CD after the last track finishes playing.

__Note:__ To turn on Repeat from the Now Playing window, press Ctrl + T.

PLAY SONGS RANDOMLY

⑪ Click the **Turn Shuffle On** button (⤨).

Windows Media Player shuffles the order of play.

__Note:__ To turn on Shuffle from the Now Playing window, press Ctrl + H.

Simplify It

My Details pane does not list the song titles. Why not?
Windows Media Player tries to gather information about the album from the Internet. If it cannot ascertain song titles, then it displays track numbers instead. To add your own titles, right-click the song title you want to change and click **Edit**. Type your text and press Enter. You can also press F2 and then Tab to edit a song title.

Is there a way to keep the Now Playing window in view at all times?
Yes. You can configure the Now Playing window so that it stays on top of any other window that you have open on your desktop. This enables you to control the playback no matter what other programs are running on your PC. Right-click the Now Playing window and then click **Always show Now Playing on top**.

Copy Tracks from a Music CD

You can add tracks from a music CD to the library in Windows Media Player. This enables you to listen to an album without having to put the CD into your CD or DVD drive each time. The process of adding tracks from a CD is called *copying,* or *ripping,* in Windows 7.

You can either rip an entire CD directly from the Now Playing window, or you can rip selected tracks using the library.

RIP AN ENTIRE CD USING THE NOW PLAYING WINDOW

1 Insert a CD into your computer's CD or DVD drive.

The Now Playing window appears.

2 Click **Rip CD** (⊙).

Media Player begins ripping the entire CD.

RIP SELECTED TRACKS USING THE LIBRARY

1 Insert a CD into your computer's CD or DVD drive.

If the Now Playing window appears, click **Switch to Library**.

● Media Player displays a list of the CD's tracks.

2 Click the CD tracks that you do not want to copy (✓ changes to ☐).

3 Click **Rip CD**.

Windows Media Player begins copying the track or tracks.

● The Rip Status column displays the copy progress.

● After each file is copied, the Rip Status column displays a Ripped to Library message.

● The copy is complete when all the tracks you selected display the Ripped to Library status.

Simplify It

I ripped a track by accident. How do I remove it from the library?
In the library, click **Music**, click **Album**, and then double-click the album that you ripped to display a list of the tracks. Right-click the track that you want to remove, and then click **Delete** from the menu that appears.

Can I adjust the quality of the copies?
Yes. You do that by changing the *bit rate*, which is a measure of how much of the CD's original data gets copied to your computer. This is measured in kilobits per second (Kbps): the higher the value the higher the quality, but the more disk space each track takes up. Click **Rip Settings**, click **Audio Quality** from the menu that appears, and then click the value you want.

Create a Playlist

You can create a custom music experience by creating your own playlist. Normally, the Windows Media Player library takes the music tracks you copy from a music CD, or the songs you store on your computer hard drive, or download from the Internet, and organizes them in preset categories, such as album, artist, and genre. For something different, you can take tracks from multiple categories and add them to a separate playlist, which enables you to play only the songs that you want to hear.

Create a Playlist

① Click **Create playlist**.

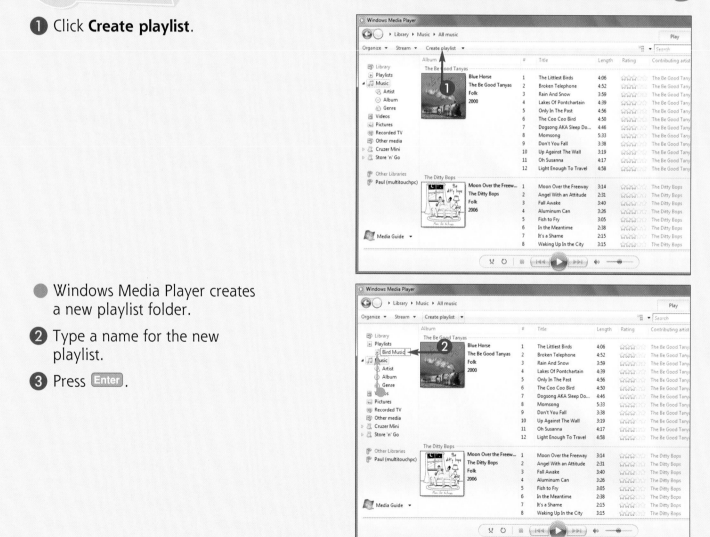

● Windows Media Player creates a new playlist folder.

② Type a name for the new playlist.

③ Press Enter.

④ Click and drag items from the library and drop them on the playlist.

⑤ Click the playlist.

The Details pane shows the songs you added.

⑥ Click and drag the songs to change the playlist order.

⑦ Click **Play** (▶) to listen to the playlist.

Can I add items to an existing playlist?

Yes, there are a couple of methods you can use. The first method is to repeat Step 4 for any other items you want to add to the playlist. The second method is to locate the song you want to add, right-click the song, click **Add to**, and then click the name of the playlist in the menu that appears.

Why does Media Player show only my most recently created playlists in the Navigation pane?

By default, Media Player's Navigation pane is configured to show only the five most recent playlists. If you prefer to see all your playlists, right-click any item in the Navigation pane and then click **Customize navigation pane**. In the Customize Navigation Pane dialog box, click the **All** check box that appears under the Playlists branch (☐ changes to ☑).

Burn Music Files to a CD

You can copy, or *burn*, music files from your computer onto a CD. Burning CDs is a great way to create customized CDs that you can listen to on the computer, in your car, through a stereo system, or in a portable device.

With Windows Media Player, you create a list of the songs that you want to add to the CD.

You then burn the music files to the CD from within the Windows Media Player window.

To burn music files to a CD with Windows Media Player, your computer must have a recordable CD or DVD drive, and you must have a blank recordable CD disc.

Burn Music Files to a CD

① Insert a blank CD into your computer's recordable CD drive.

② Click the **Burn** tab.

● The Burn list appears.

③ Click and drag items from the library and drop them inside the Burn list.

④ Repeat Step **3** to add more files to the Burn list.

Windows Media Player adds the files to the Burn list.

Windows Media Player updates the approximate time remaining on the disc.

5 Click **Start burn**.

Windows Media Player converts the files to CD tracks and copies them to the CD.

The Burn tab shows the progress of the burn.

Note: *When the recording is complete, Windows Media Player automatically ejects the disc. Do not attempt to eject the disc yourself before the burn is finished.*

Simplify It

Do I have to burn the songs in the order they appear in the list?
No, Media Player offers several options for rearranging the tracks before burning. Perhaps the easiest method is to click and drag a track and then drop it in the list location you prefer. You can also click **Burn options** (⊡▾) and then click either **Shuffle list** or **Sort list by** and then click a sort order.

What happens if I have more music than can fit on a single disc?
You can still add all the music you want to burn to the Burn list. Windows Media Player fills the first disc and then starts on a second disk (look for Disc 2 in the Burn list). After the program finishes burning the first disc, it prompts you to insert the next one.

Play a DVD

You can use Windows Media Player to play DVDs. Windows Media Player enables you to watch any multimedia items stored on a DVD, such as movies and video footage.

Depending on how you set up your DVD drive and Windows Media Player, your DVD may begin playing as soon as you insert it. If it does not, you can follow the steps in this section to initiate playback.

Play a DVD

1 Insert a DVD into your computer's DVD drive.

2 In Windows Media Player, click the DVD in the Navigation pane.

3 Click **Play** ().

● Windows Media Player plays the DVD and displays the DVD's menu.

DVD menu items can vary in appearance and use different layouts.

4 Click the menu item or feature you want to access.

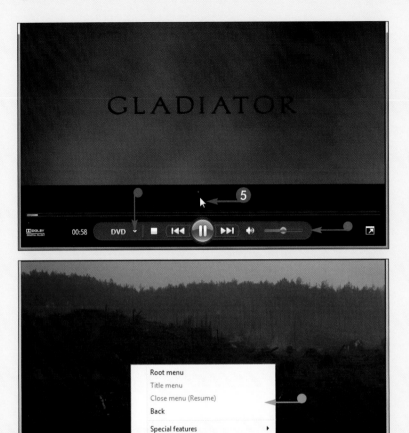

Windows Media Player begins playback.

⑤ To control playback, position the mouse ⌖ within the DVD window.

● Media Player displays the playback controls.

● You can click the **DVD** ⊡ to see a list of DVD options.

● You can use the DVD options to return to the main menu, select special features, and display the DVD full-screen.

Simplify It

Can I restrict the DVDs my kids watch?
Yes. First, set up your kids with Standard user accounts (Chapter 7). Then, in Windows Media Player:

① Click **Organize** and then click **Options**.

② In the Options dialog box, click the **DVD** tab.

③ Click **Change**.

④ In the Change Rating Restriction dialog box, click ⊡ and then click the maximum rating you want.

⑤ Click **OK**, and click **OK** in the Options dialog box.

Navigate a DVD

You can control how a DVD plays by using the various navigation controls in the Windows Media Player window. The window includes volume and playback controls. You can also navigate to different scenes using the list of tracks in the Playlist pane. All scenes, or tracks, stem from a root menu that directs you to the DVD's contents.

Throughout this section, note that you must position the mouse within the DVD window to display the playback controls.

Navigate a DVD

STOP AND START A DVD

① Click the **Stop** button (■).

Windows Media Player stops the DVD playback.

② Click the **Play** button (▶).

Windows Media Player restarts the playback from the beginning.

You can also click the **Pause** button (❚❚) to pause the playback if you want to resume playing in the same scene.

NAVIGATE SCENES

① Click the **Previous** button (◄◄).

Windows Media Player jumps to the previous scene.

② Click the **Next** button (►►).

Windows Media Player jumps to the next scene.

● You can also rewind or fast-forward the DVD by clicking and dragging the **Seek** slider.

RETURN TO THE ROOT MENU

1️⃣ Click the **DVD** ⬝.

2️⃣ Click **Root menu**.

The DVD's opening menu appears in the Windows Media Player window.

![Simplify It]

What is a root menu?
The *root menu* is the opening menu of a DVD, and it typically displays links to the various segments, features, or clips on the DVD. You can return to the root menu at any time to access other DVD elements. On full-screen view, you can quickly access the root menu with a shortcut menu. Right-click over the DVD screen, click **DVD features**, and then click **Root menu**.

Can I adjust the DVD's play speed?
Yes, you can choose from three settings: Slow, Normal, or Fast. The Slow setting plays the DVD in slow motion. The Normal setting plays the DVD at normal speed. The Fast setting accelerates the play. To change the play speed, right-click the **Play** button (▶), and then click **Slow playback** (or press Ctrl + Shift + S), **Normal playback** (or press Ctrl + Shift + N), or **Fast playback** (or press Ctrl + Shift + G).

Chapter 6

Working with Files

This chapter shows you how to work with the files on your computer. These easy and efficient methods show you how to perform the most common file tasks, including viewing files, selecting files, copying and moving files, and renaming files. In this chapter you also learn how to burn files to a recordable CD or DVD disc and how to create new folders to hold your files. You also learn how to delete a file that you no longer need, as well as how to restore a file that you deleted accidentally. Finally, you also learn how to use Windows 7's powerful search feature to help you locate the file you need.

View Your Files

You can view the files you create, as well as those stored on your hard drive that you download and copy to your computer. All your files are stored in folders on your computer's hard drive. Some of your files will be in the main libraries that are part of your user profile —

including Documents, Music, and Pictures — but you may have other files within subfolders of those libraries.

If you want to open or work with those files, you first need to open the appropriate library or subfolder to view them.

View Your Files

① Click **Start**.

② Click your user name.

Windows 7 displays your user folder.

③ Double-click the folder you want to view.

Windows 7 displays the contents of the folder including subfolders.

④ If the files you want to view are stored in a subfolder, double-click the subfolder.

Windows 7 displays the contents of the subfolder.

Simplify It

How do I view the files I have on a CD, Flash drive, memory card, or other media?
Insert the media into the appropriate drive or slot on your computer. If you see the AutoPlay window, click **Open folder to view files**. Otherwise, click **Start** and then click **Computer** to display the Computer window, and then double-click the disk drive or device that contains the files you want to view. Windows 7 displays the contents of the media.

What is a file library?
In Windows 7, the four main document storage areas — Documents, Music, Pictures, and Videos — are set up as *libraries*, where each library consists of two or more folders. For example, the Documents library consists of your My Documents folder and the Public Documents folder. To add a folder to a library, click the **locations** link and then click **Add**.

Select a File

Whether you want to rename a file, make a copy of a file, move several files to a new location, or delete some files, you first have to select the file or files so that Windows 7 knows exactly the ones you want to work with.

Although you learn specifically about selecting files in this section, the technique for selecting folders is exactly the same.

SELECT A SINGLE FILE

1 Open the folder containing the file.

2 Click the file.

SELECT MULTIPLE FILES

1 Open the folder containing the files.

2 Click the first file you want to select.

3 Press and hold Ctrl and click each of the other files you want to select.

SELECT A GROUP OF FILES

① Open the folder containing the files.

② Position the mouse ⬚ slightly above and slightly to the left of the first file in the group.

③ Click and drag the mouse ⬚ down and to the right until all the files in the group are selected.

SELECT ALL FILES

① Open the folder containing the files.

② Click **Organize**.

③ Click **Select all**.

● Windows Explorer selects all the files in the folder.

Note: *A quick way to select all the files in a folder is to press* Ctrl + A .

How do I deselect a file?
● To deselect a single file from a multiple-file selection, press and hold Ctrl and click the file you want to deselect.
● To deselect all files, click an empty area within the folder.
● To reverse the selection — deselect the selected files and select the deselected files — press Alt , click **Edit**, and then click **Invert Selection**.

Change the File View

You can configure how Windows 7 displays the files in a folder by changing the file view. This enables you to see larger or smaller icons or the details of each file.

Choose a view such as Small Icons to see more files in the folder window. For files that show preview thumbnails instead of icons — such as

pictures and videos — choose a view such as Large Icons or Extra Large Icons to get a better look at the thumbnails.

If you want to see more information about the files, choose either the Tiles view or Details view.

Change the File View

1 Open the folder containing the files you want to view.

2 Click the **Views** ⊡ to open the Views list.

3 Click the view you want.

● The slider points to the current view. You can also click and drag the slider to select a view.

● Windows Explorer changes the file view (to Tiles, in this example).

Preview a File

Windows 7 enables you to view the contents of some files without opening them. This makes it easier to select the file you want to work with.

One way to preview a file is to switch to a view that shows preview thumbnails, such as Large Icons or Extra Large Icons. (See the section "Change the File View," earlier in this chapter.)

However, to get a larger preview, and to preview a wider variety of file types, you need to open Windows Explorer's Preview pane.

Windows 7 previews only certain types of files, such as text documents, rich text documents, Web pages, images, and videos.

Preview a File

① Open the folder containing the file you want to preview.

② Click the **Preview pane** icon (▤).

● The Preview pane appears.

● The file's contents appear in the Preview pane.

● You can click and drag the left border of the Preview pane to change its size.

● When you are finished with the Preview pane, click ▤ to close it.

Copy a File

You can make an exact copy of a file, which is useful if you want to make a backup of an important file on a flash drive, memory card, or other removable disk, or if you want to send the copy on a disk to another person.

This section shows you how to copy a single file, but the steps also work if you select multiple files, as described earlier in this chapter in the "Select a File" section. You can also use these steps to copy a folder.

Copy a File

① Open the folder containing the file you want to copy.

② Select the file.

③ Click **Organize**.

④ Click **Copy**.

Windows 7 places a copy of the file in a special memory location called the *clipboard*.

⑤ Open the location you want to use to store the copy.

⑥ Click **Organize**.

⑦ Click **Paste**.

● Windows 7 inserts a copy of the file in the location.

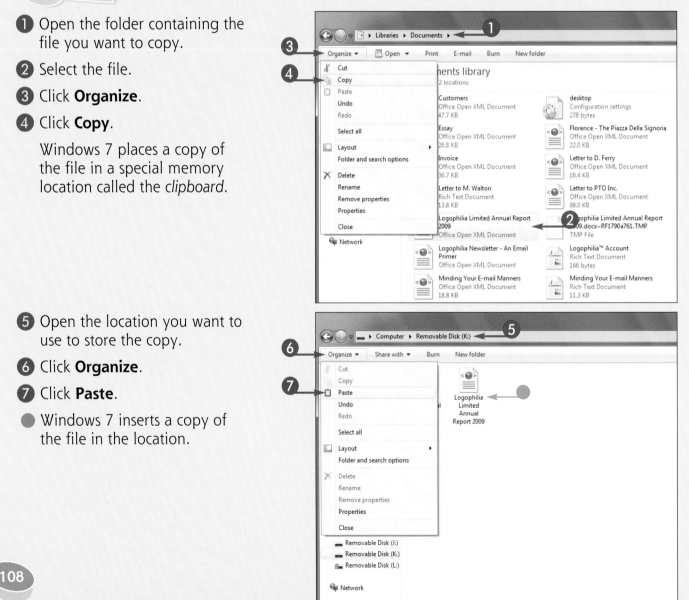

Move a File

When you need to store a file in a new location, the easiest way is to move the file from its current folder to another folder on your computer.

This section shows you how to move a single file, but the steps also work if you select multiple files, as described earlier in this chapter in the "Select a File" section. You can also use these steps to move a folder.

Move a File

1 Open the folder containing the file you want to move.

2 Select the file.

3 Click **Organize**.

4 Click **Cut**.

Windows 7 removes the file from the folder and places it in a special memory location called the *clipboard*.

5 Click the new location you want to use for the file.

6 Click **Organize**.

7 Click **Paste**.

Windows 7 inserts the file in the new location.

Burn Files to a CD or DVD

If your computer has a recordable CD or DVD drive, you can copy — or *burn* — files and folders to a recordable disc. This enables you to store a large amount of data in a single place for convenient transport, storage, or backup.

To burn files, your computer must have a recordable CD or DVD drive, and you must have a blank recordable CD or DVD disc.

If you want to copy music files to a CD, see the "Burn Music Files to a CD" section in Chapter 5.

Burn Files to a CD or DVD

1 Insert a recordable disc into your recordable CD or DVD drive.

The AutoPlay dialog box appears.

2 Click **Burn files to disc**.

If you have never used the disc for burning files, the Burn a Disc dialog box appears.

3 Type a title for the disc.

4 Click **Like a USB flash drive** (◎ changes to ◉).

5 Click **Next**.

Windows 7 formats the disc and displays a dialog box to show you the progress.

When the format is complete, the AutoPlay dialog box appears.

6 Click **Close** (⊠).

7 Open the folder containing the files you want to copy to the disc.

8 Select the files.

● If you selected more than 15 files and you want to see the total size of the selection, first click **Show more details**.

![Simplify It]

Does it matter what type of recordable CD or DVD I use?
Not in Windows 7. Normally, CD-R and DVD-R discs allow you to copy files to the disc only once. After you finalize the disc, it is locked and you cannot copy more files to the disc, or deletes files from the disc. However, Windows 7 uses a new system that enables you to copy, recopy, and delete files with any type of recordable disc.

How much data can I store on a recordable CD?
Most recordable CDs can hold about 650MB (megabytes) of information. If a typical word processing document is about 50KB (kilobytes), this means you can store about 13,000 files on a recordable CD. For larger files, such as images, you can store about 650 1MB files on the disc.

Burn Files to a CD or DVD *(continued)*

With Windows 7's new method for burning files to a CD or DVD, you only need to format the disc once. After that, you can burn more files to the disc, delete files from the disc, and generally work with the disc just like you would a regular folder on your hard drive.

When you have finished working with the disc, you must close the recording session to allow Windows 7 to set up the disc for use on other computers and devices.

Burn Files to a CD or DVD *(continued)*

● If you clicked Show More Details, the Size number shows the total size of the selected files.

9 Click **Burn**.

> **Note:** *If you want to copy everything in the folder to the disc, do not select any file or folder and click **Burn**.*

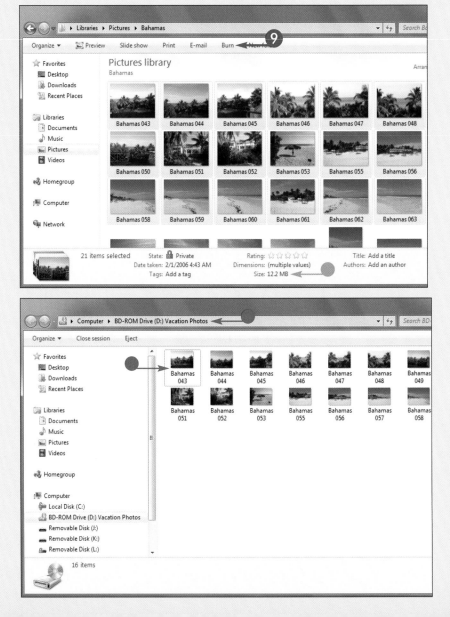

Windows 7 burns the files to the disc.

● Windows 7 opens the disc and displays the copied files.

10 Repeat Steps **7** to **9** to burn more files to the disc.

① Open the disc folder.

② Click **Close session**.

Windows 7 closes the disc session to allow the disc to be used on other computers.

● This message appears while the disc is being closed.

③ When the Closing Session message disappears, click **Eject**.

Windows 7 ejects the disc.

Simplify It

I want to start over with a CD-RW or DVD-RW disc. Is there an easy way to erase the disc?

Yes. Follow these steps:

① Click **Start**.

② Click **Computer**.

③ Right-click the disc icon.

④ Click **Format**.

The Format dialog box appears.

⑤ Type a new name for the disc, if desired.

⑥ Click **Start**.

Windows 7 warns you that all data on the disc will be erased.

⑦ Click **OK**.

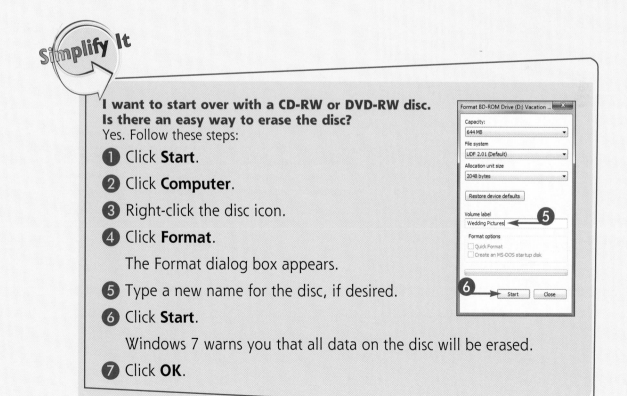

Rename a File

You can change the names of your files, which is useful if the current name of the file does not accurately describe its contents. By giving your documents descriptive names, you make it easier to later find the file you want.

Make sure that you rename only those documents that you have created yourself or that someone else has given to you. Do not rename any of the Windows 7 system files or any files associated with your programs, or your computer may behave erratically or crash.

Rename a File

① Open the folder that contains the file you want to rename.

② Click the file.

③ Click **Organize**.

Note: In addition to renaming files, you can also rename any folders that you created yourself.

④ Click **Rename**.

A text box appears around the file name.

Note: You can also select the Rename command by clicking the file and then pressing F2.

⑤ Type the new name you want to use for the file.

Note: If you decide that you do not want to rename the file after all, press Esc to cancel the operation.

Note: The name you type can be up to 255 characters long, but it cannot include the following characters: < > , ? : " \ *.

⑥ Press Enter or click an empty section of the folder.

The new name appears under the file's icon.

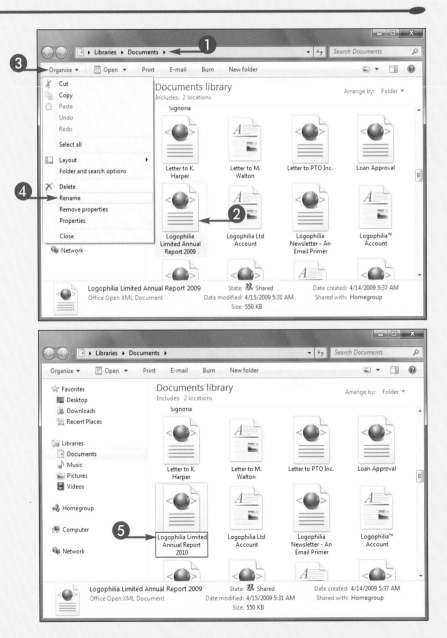

Create a New File

You can quickly create a new file directly within a file folder. You normally create a new file by opening the appropriate programs, pulling down the File menu, and then choosing the New command, as explained in the "Create a Document" section in Chapter 3. However, creating a new file directly within a folder is faster, and often more convenient, than running a program's New command because you do not need to open a program to create the file.

Create a New File

1 Open the folder in which you want to create the file.

2 Right-click an empty section of the folder.

3 Click **New**.

4 Click the type of file you want to create.

Note: If you click **Folder**, Windows 7 creates a new subfolder.

Note: The New menu on your system may contain more items than you see here because some programs install their own file types.

An icon for the new file appears in the folder.

5 Type the name you want to use for the new file.

6 Press Enter.

Delete a File

When you have a file that you no longer need, instead of leaving the file to clutter your hard drive, you can delete it.

Make sure that you delete only those documents that you have created yourself or that someone else has given to you. Do not delete any of the Windows 7 system files or any files associated with your programs, or your computer may behave erratically or crash.

If you happen to delete a file accidentally, you can usually recover it; see the section "Restore a Deleted File," later in this chapter.

Delete a File

① Open the folder that contains the file you want to delete.

② Click the file you want to delete.

Note: *If you need to remove more than one file, select all the files you want to delete.*

③ Click **Organize**.

④ Click **Delete**.

Note: *Another way to select the Delete command is to press* ⌈Delete⌉.

The Delete File dialog box appears.

⑤ Click **Yes**.

The file disappears from the folder.

Note: *Another way to delete a file is to click and drag it to the desktop's Recycle Bin icon.*

Restore a
Deleted File

If you delete a file in error, Windows 7 enables you to restore the file by placing it back in the folder from which you deleted it.

You can restore a deleted file because Windows 7 moves each deleted file from its original

folder to a special folder called the Recycle Bin, where the file stays for a few days or a few weeks, depending on how often you empty the Recycle Bin or how full the folder becomes.

Restore a Deleted File

1 Double-click the desktop **Recycle Bin** icon.

The Recycle Bin folder appears.

2 Click the file you want to restore.

3 Click **Restore this item**.

The file disappears from the Recycle Bin and reappears in its original folder.

Search for a File

After you have used your computer for a while and have created many documents, you might have trouble locating a specific file. This is particularly true if you use your computer frequently, because you might have thousands of your own files stored in various folders throughout the hard drive. You can save a great deal of time by having Windows 7 search for your document.

Windows 7 searches not only for documents, but also for e-mail messages, contacts, Internet Explorer favorites, applications, and more.

You can search from the Start menu or use the Search box in a folder window.

Search for a File

SEARCH FROM THE START MENU

1 Click **Start**.

2 Click the Search box.

3 Type your search text.

● As you type, Windows 7 displays the programs, documents, and other data on your system with a name that matches your search text.

4 If you see the program or document you want, click it to open it.

SEARCH FROM A FOLDER WINDOW

1 Open the folder in which you want to search.

2 Click the Search box.

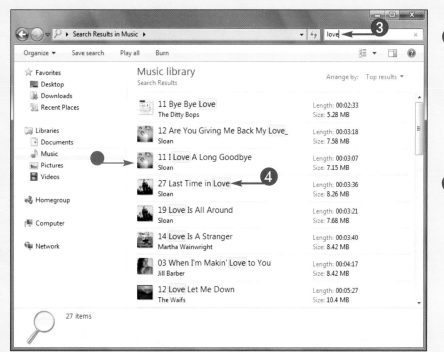

③ Type your search text.

● As you type, Windows 7 displays the folders and documents in the current folder with names, contents, or keywords that match your search text.

④ If you see the folder or document you want, double-click it to open it.

Simplify It

I want to run the same search frequently. Can I save it?
Yes, follow these steps:

① Run the search you want to save.

② Click **Save Search**.

The Save As dialog box appears.

③ Type a file name for the search.

④ Click **Save**.

● Windows 7 saves the search file in the Favorites area. Click the file to rerun your search.

Chapter 7

Sharing Your Computer with Others

If you share your computer with other people, you can create separate user accounts so that each person works only with his own documents, programs, and Windows 7 settings. This chapter shows you how to view and create user accounts, log on and off different accounts, change a user's name and picture, and delete accounts you no longer need.

In this chapter you also learn about Windows 7's new homegroup feature, which makes it easy to share documents, music, photos, and other files with people on your network. You learn how to create a new homegroup and join an existing homegroup.

Display User Accounts

To create, change, or delete user accounts, you need to display Windows 7's Manage Accounts window.

If you share your computer with other people, you can run into problems because each person wants his own programs, documents, and settings. To solve these problems, you can create a separate user account for each person. A *user account* is a kind of profile that Windows 7 maintains for a single person. That profile gives each user his own collection of folders and settings, and allows each user to install his own programs. When a person logs into his account, he does not see the profile of any other user.

Display User Accounts

① Click **Start**.

② Click **Control Panel**.

The Control Panel window appears.

③ Click **Add or remove user accounts**.

Note: If the User Account Control dialog box appears, click **Continue** or type an administrator password and click **Submit**.

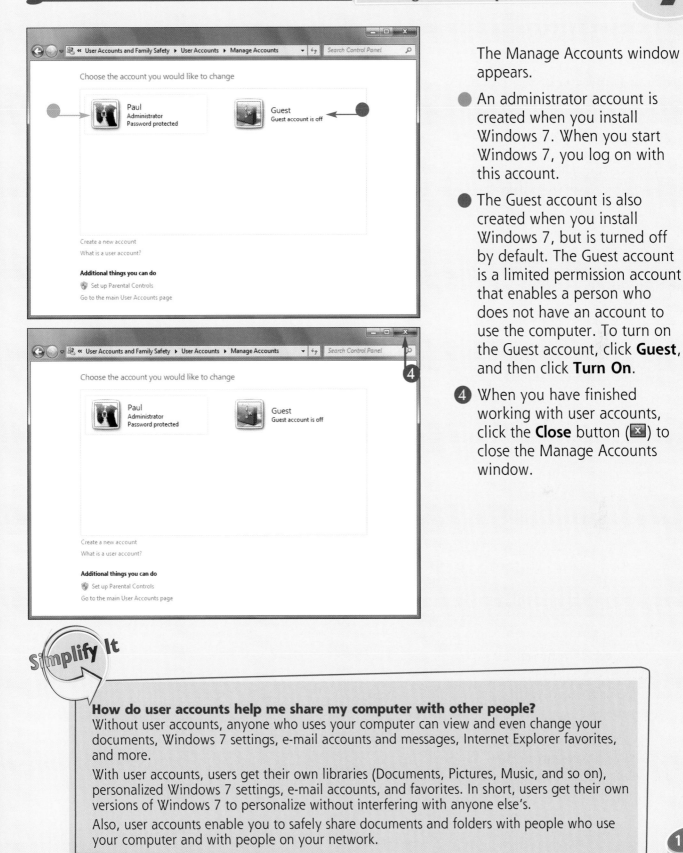

The Manage Accounts window appears.

● An administrator account is created when you install Windows 7. When you start Windows 7, you log on with this account.

● The Guest account is also created when you install Windows 7, but is turned off by default. The Guest account is a limited permission account that enables a person who does not have an account to use the computer. To turn on the Guest account, click **Guest**, and then click **Turn On**.

④ When you have finished working with user accounts, click the **Close** button (☒) to close the Manage Accounts window.

Simplify It

How do user accounts help me share my computer with other people?

Without user accounts, anyone who uses your computer can view and even change your documents, Windows 7 settings, e-mail accounts and messages, Internet Explorer favorites, and more.

With user accounts, users get their own libraries (Documents, Pictures, Music, and so on), personalized Windows 7 settings, e-mail accounts, and favorites. In short, users get their own versions of Windows 7 to personalize without interfering with anyone else's.

Also, user accounts enable you to safely share documents and folders with people who use your computer and with people on your network.

Create a User Account

If you want to share your computer with another person, you need to create a user account for that individual. To create a new account, you specify a unique name and an optional password. If you supply a password with an account, then only people who know that password can access the account's files, programs, and settings. This is an excellent security precaution, so you should safeguard each account with a password.

Note that you must be logged on to Windows 7 with an administrator account or know an administrator's password to create a user account.

Create a User Account

CREATE A USER ACCOUNT

① Display the Manage Accounts window.

Note: See "Display User Accounts," earlier in this chapter to learn how to display the Manage Accounts window.

② Click **Create a new account**.

The Create New Account window appears.

③ Type the name you want to use for the new account.

④ Click the account type you want (◎ changes to ◉).

Note: See the tip on the following page to learn the difference between the two account types.

⑤ Click **Create Account**.

Windows 7 creates the user account.

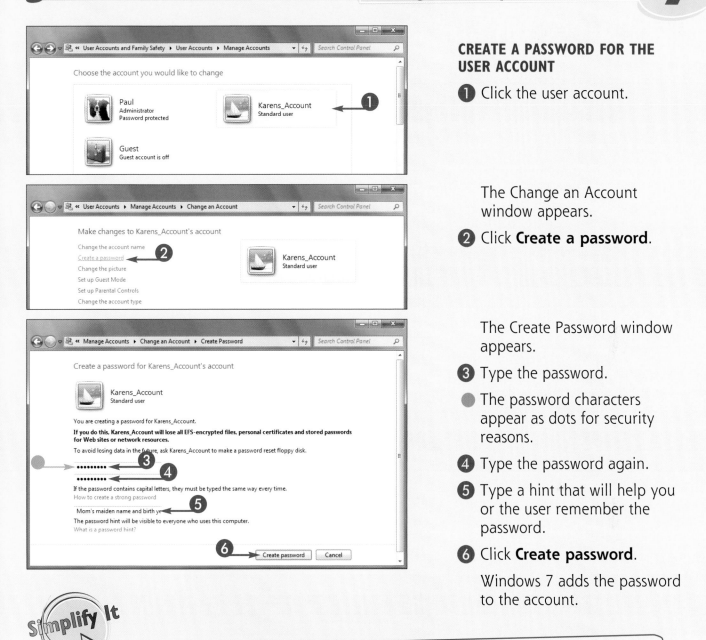

CREATE A PASSWORD FOR THE USER ACCOUNT

1 Click the user account.

The Change an Account window appears.

2 Click **Create a password**.

The Create Password window appears.

3 Type the password.

● The password characters appear as dots for security reasons.

4 Type the password again.

5 Type a hint that will help you or the user remember the password.

6 Click **Create password**.

Windows 7 adds the password to the account.

Simplify It

How do I decide what type of account to give each user?
The two different account types — administrator and standard — affect the extent to which the user can interact with the computer:

● An administrator has complete access to the computer, including access to all users' documents. Administrators can also install programs and devices and add, change, and delete user accounts.

● Standard users have partial access to the computer. They can access only their own documents, as well as any documents that other users have designated to share. Standard users can modify only their own settings, and can change some aspects of their user accounts, including their passwords and pictures.

Switch Between Accounts

After you have created more than one account on your computer, you can switch between accounts. This is useful when one person is already working in Windows 7 and another person needs to use the computer.

One way to do this would be to have the current user log off and then have the other user log on. This works, but it is often inconvenient, particularly if the original user

wants to resume working when the other user is finished with the computer.

To avoid this problem, you can switch from one account to another. In this case, Windows 7 leaves the original user's programs and windows running so that after the second person is finished, the original user can log on again and continue working as before.

Switch Between Accounts

1 Click **Start**.

● The current user's name and picture appear on the Start menu.

2 Click the power button arrow (▶) to display the menu.

3 Click **Switch user**.

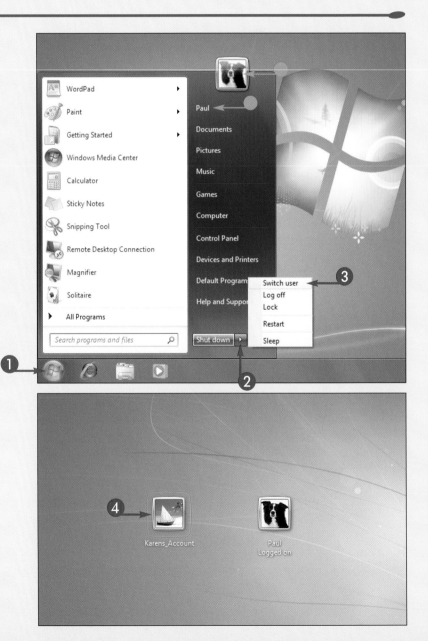

The Welcome screen appears.

4 Click the user account you want to switch to.

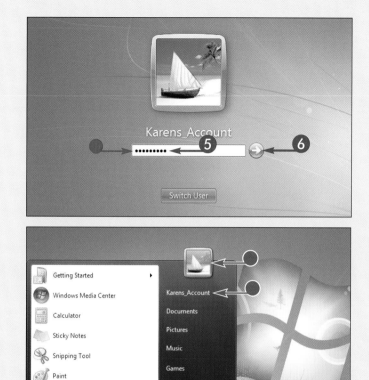

● If the account is protected by a password, the password box appears.

Note: See "Protect an Account with a Password" in Chapter 10 for details on protecting an account with a password.

⑤ Type the password.

⑥ Click the **Go** button (◉).

⑦ Click **Start**.

● The user's name and picture now appear in the Start menu.

Simplify It

What happens if I forget my password?
When you set up your password as described in the previous section, Windows 7 asks you to supply a hint to help you remember the password. If you cannot remember your password, follow these steps:

❶ Type anything into the password box.

❷ Click the **Go** button (◉).

Windows 7 tells you the password is incorrect.

❸ Click **OK** to return to the Welcome screen.

● Windows 7 displays the password hint.

Change a User's Name

If the user name you are using now is not suitable for some reason, you can change it to a different name. If you are running Windows 7 under an administrator account, then you can also change the name of any other user on the system.

When you change the user's name, you are changing the name that appears on the Start menu, in the Manage Accounts window, and on the Windows 7 Welcome screen.

Change a User's Name

1 Display the Manage Accounts window.

Note: *See "Display User Accounts," earlier in this chapter, to learn how to display the Manage Accounts window.*

2 Click the user account you want to work with.

The Change an Account window appears.

3 Click **Change the account name**.

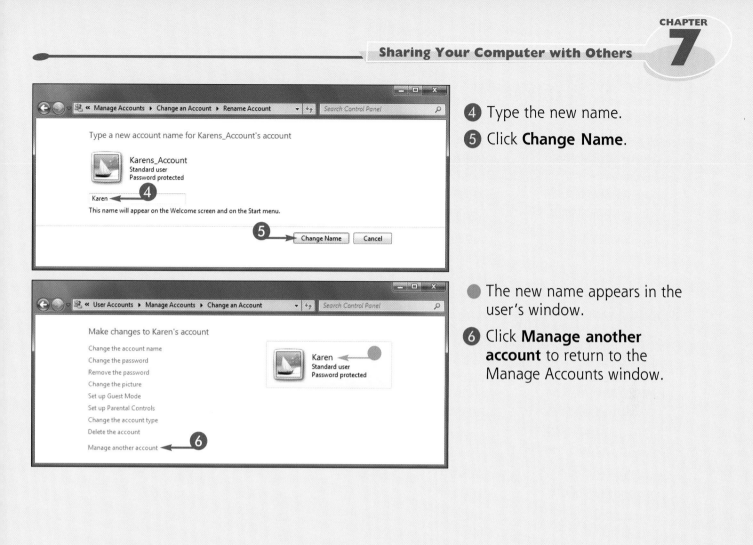

④ Type the new name.

⑤ Click **Change Name**.

● The new name appears in the user's window.

⑥ Click **Manage another account** to return to the Manage Accounts window.

Simplify It

Are there any restrictions in the names I can use?
Yes, you have to watch out for the following:

● The name cannot be any longer than 20 characters.

● The name cannot include any of the following characters: , < > / ? ; : " [ ] \
| = + *

● The name cannot be the same as the computer's name. To check the computer name, click **Start**, click **Control Panel**, click **System and Security**, and then click **See the name of this computer**. In the System window, look for the Computer Name setting.

Change a User's Picture

Windows 7 assigns a random picture to each new user account, and this picture appears in the Manage Accounts window, the Welcome screen, and on the Start menu. If you do not like your picture, or if you have a more suitable picture that you would prefer to use, you can change your picture. You can either use one of the three dozen pictures that Windows 7 provides, or you can use one of your own pictures, such as a photo or drawing.

Change a User's Picture

① Display the Manage Accounts window.

Note: See "Display User Accounts," earlier in this chapter, to learn how to display the Manage Accounts window.

② Click the user account you want to work with.

The Change an Account window appears.

③ Click **Change the picture**.

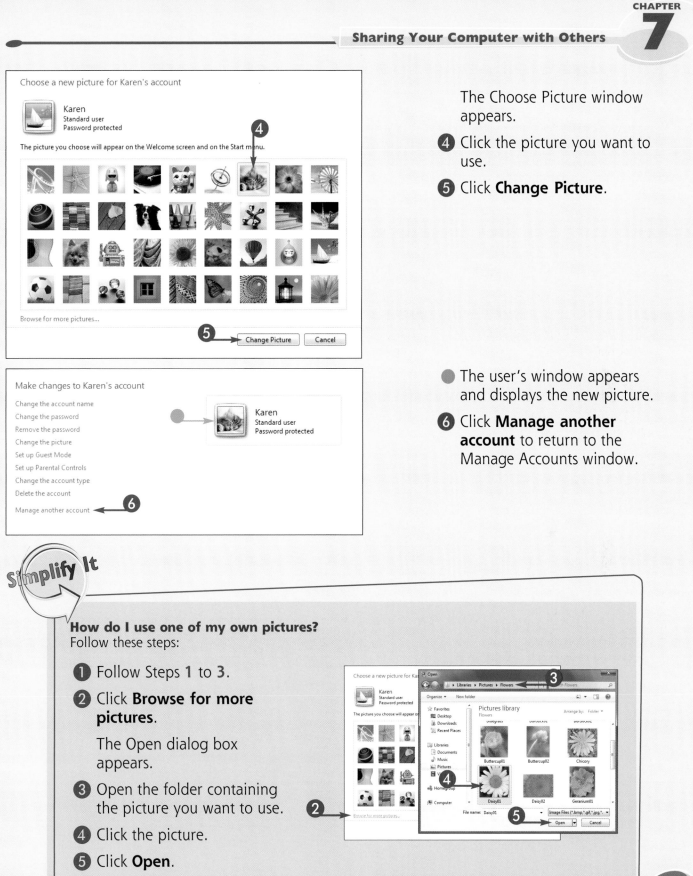

Choose a new picture for Karen's account

Karen
Standard user
Password protected

The picture you choose will appear on the Welcome screen and on the Start menu.

Browse for more pictures...

Change Picture   Cancel

Make changes to Karen's account

Change the account name
Change the password
Remove the password
Change the picture
Set up Guest Mode
Set up Parental Controls
Change the account type
Delete the account

Manage another account

Karen
Standard user
Password protected

The Choose Picture window appears.

④ Click the picture you want to use.

⑤ Click **Change Picture**.

● The user's window appears and displays the new picture.

⑥ Click **Manage another account** to return to the Manage Accounts window.

How do I use one of my own pictures?
Follow these steps:

① Follow Steps **1** to **3**.

② Click **Browse for more pictures**.

The Open dialog box appears.

③ Open the folder containing the picture you want to use.

④ Click the picture.

⑤ Click **Open**.

Choose a new picture for Kar...

Karen
Standard user
Password protected

The picture you choose will appear on...

Libraries ▸ Pictures ▸ Flowers

Organize ▾   New folder

Favorites
  Desktop
  Downloads
  Recent Places

Libraries
  Documents
  Music
  Pictures
  V...
HomeGroup
Computer

Pictures library
Flowers

Buttercup01   Buttercup02   Chicory

Daisy01   Daisy02   Geranium01

File name: Daisy01   Image Files (*.bmp,*.gif,*.jpg,*...

Open   Cancel

Delete an Account

You can delete a user's account when it is no longer needed. This reduces the number of users in the Manage Accounts window and on the Welcome screen, which makes those screens easier to navigate.

Deleting an account can also free up some disk space. When you delete an account, Windows 7 asks if you want to keep the user's files on the computer, including the user's documents, music, pictures, and video. If you choose not to keep those files, Windows 7 deletes them from the hard drive, thus freeing up the disk space they used.

Delete an Account

1 Display the Manage Accounts window.

Note: See "Display User Accounts," earlier in this chapter, to learn how to display the Manage Accounts window.

2 Click the user account you want to delete.

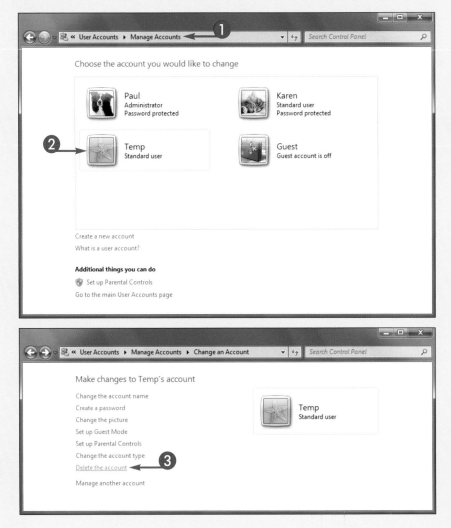

The Change an Account window appears.

3 Click **Delete the account**.

The Delete Account window appears.

④ Click to specify whether you want to keep or delete the user's personal files.

Note: See the tip, below, to learn the difference between these two options.

The Confirm Deletion window appears.

⑤ Click **Delete Account**.

Windows 7 deletes the account.

Simplify It

My user account does not offer the Delete the Account task. Why not?	**What is the difference between the Keep Files and Delete Files options?**
If yours is the only computer administrator account left on the computer, Windows 7 does not allow you to delete it. Windows 7 requires that there always be at least one computer administrator account on the computer.	The options enable you to handle user files two ways: ● Click **Keep Files** to retain the user's personal files — the contents of his or her Documents folder and desktop. These files are saved on your desktop in a folder named after the user. All other personal items — settings, e-mail accounts and messages, and Internet Explorer favorites — are deleted. ● Click **Delete Files** to delete all of the user's personal files, settings, messages, and favorites.

Create a Homegroup

You can share documents and media easily with other Windows 7 computers by creating a homegroup on your network. A homegroup simplifies network sharing by making it easy to create a homegroup and share documents, pictures, music, videos, and even printers.

You use one Windows 7 computer to create the homegroup, and Windows 7 assigns a password for that homegroup. You then use the password to join your other Windows 7 computers to the homegroup. See "Join a Homegroup," later in this chapter.

Create a Homegroup

① Click **Start**.

② Click **Documents**.

The Documents library appears.

③ Click **Homegroup**.

④ Click **Create a homegroup**.

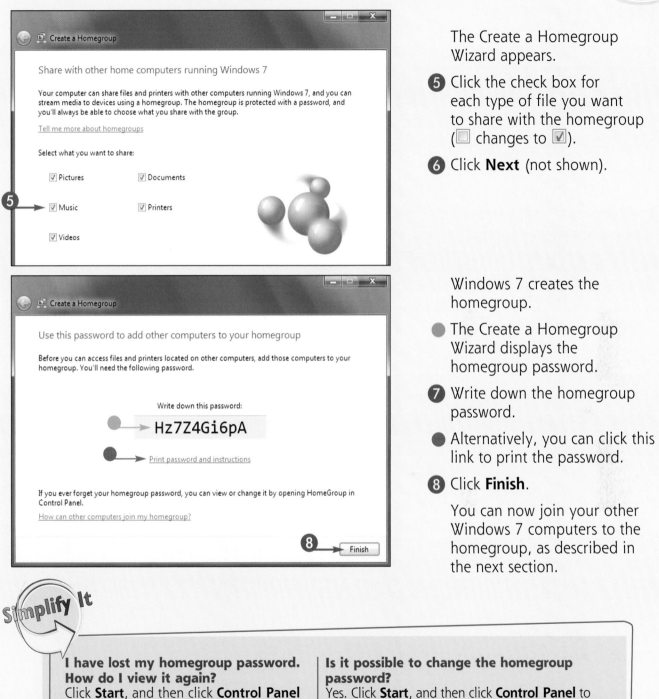

The Create a Homegroup Wizard appears.

⑤ Click the check box for each type of file you want to share with the homegroup (☐ changes to ☑).

⑥ Click **Next** (not shown).

Windows 7 creates the homegroup.

● The Create a Homegroup Wizard displays the homegroup password.

⑦ Write down the homegroup password.

● Alternatively, you can click this link to print the password.

⑧ Click **Finish**.

You can now join your other Windows 7 computers to the homegroup, as described in the next section.

Simplify It

I have lost my homegroup password. How do I view it again?
Click **Start**, and then click **Control Panel** to open the Control Panel window. Under the Network and Internet heading, click **Choose homegroup and sharing options** to open the Homegroup window. Click the **View or print homegroup password** link to see your password. To print the password, click **Print this page**.

Is it possible to change the homegroup password?
Yes. Click **Start**, and then click **Control Panel** to open the Control Panel window. Under the Network and Internet heading, click **Choose homegroup and sharing options** to open the Homegroup window. Click the **Change the password** link and then click **Change the password** to generate a new homegroup password. If one or more computers have already joined the homegroup, you need to provide them with the new password.

Join a Homegroup

If a homegroup is on your network, you can join your Windows 7 computer to that homegroup. This enables you to access shared resources on other homegroup computers. You can also share your own resources with the homegroup, and Windows 7 lets you choose the specific types of files you want to share:

documents, pictures, music, or videos. You can also share your printer with the homegroup.

This section assumes you have already set up a homegroup as described in the "Create a Homegroup" section and that you have the homegroup password.

Join a Homegroup

① Click **Start**.

② Click **Documents**.

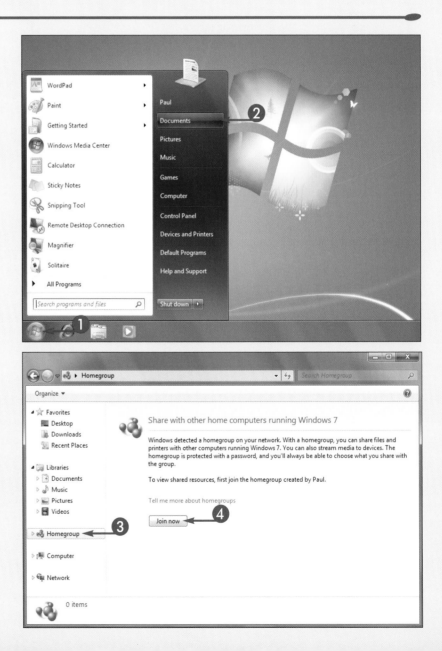

The Documents library appears.

③ Click **Homegroup**.

④ Click **Join now**.

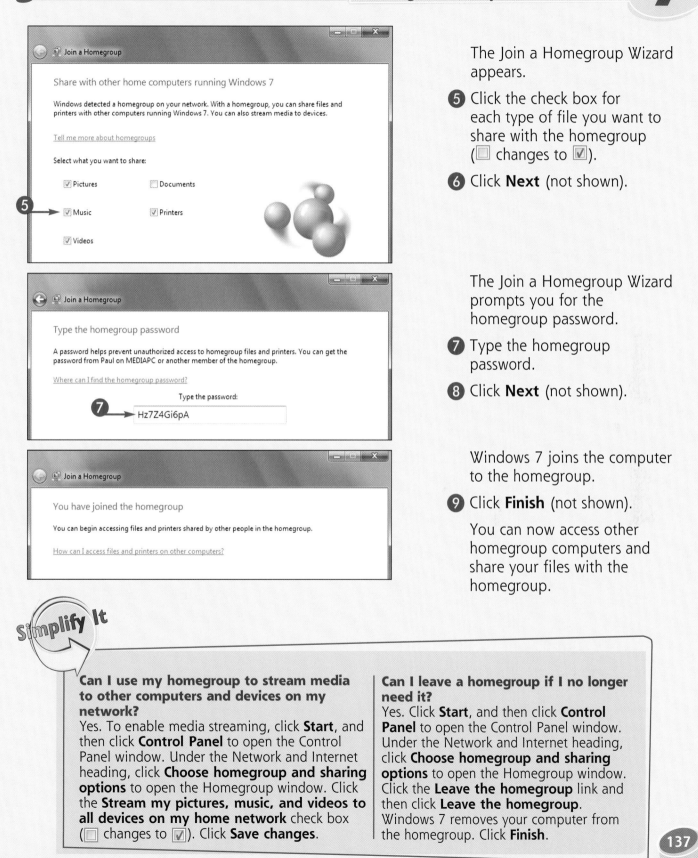

The Join a Homegroup Wizard appears.

⑤ Click the check box for each type of file you want to share with the homegroup (☐ changes to ☑).

⑥ Click **Next** (not shown).

The Join a Homegroup Wizard prompts you for the homegroup password.

⑦ Type the homegroup password.

⑧ Click **Next** (not shown).

Windows 7 joins the computer to the homegroup.

⑨ Click **Finish** (not shown).

You can now access other homegroup computers and share your files with the homegroup.

Simplify It

Can I use my homegroup to stream media to other computers and devices on my network?
Yes. To enable media streaming, click **Start**, and then click **Control Panel** to open the Control Panel window. Under the Network and Internet heading, click **Choose homegroup and sharing options** to open the Homegroup window. Click the **Stream my pictures, music, and videos to all devices on my home network** check box (☐ changes to ☑). Click **Save changes**.

Can I leave a homegroup if I no longer need it?
Yes. Click **Start**, and then click **Control Panel** to open the Control Panel window. Under the Network and Internet heading, click **Choose homegroup and sharing options** to open the Homegroup window. Click the **Leave the homegroup** link and then click **Leave the homegroup**. Windows 7 removes your computer from the homegroup. Click **Finish**.

Connect to a Wireless Network

If you have a wireless access point in your home or office, and you have a wireless network adapter installed on your computer, you can connect to the access point to access your network. If your wireless access point is connected to the Internet, then connecting to the wireless network gives your computer Internet access, as well.

Most wireless networks are protected with a security key, which is a kind of password. If your wireless network requires a security key, be sure you know the key before attempting to connect.

Connect to a Wireless Network

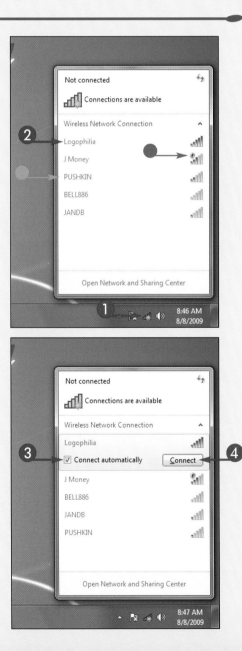

1 Click the **Network** icon (■) in the taskbar's notification area.

● Windows 7 displays a list of wireless networks in your area.

● Windows 7 displays the Unsecured icon (■) for networks not protected by a security key.

2 Click your network.

3 To have Windows 7 connect to your network automatically in the future, click to activate the **Connect automatically** check box (☐ changes to ☑).

4 Click **Connect**.

If the network is protected by a security key, Windows 7 asks you to enter it.

⑤ Type the security key.

● If you are worried that someone nearby might see the security key, you can click **Hide characters** (☐ changes to ☑) to display the characters you type as dots.

⑥ Click **OK**.

Windows 7 connects to the network.

● The network icon changes from ▨ to ▥ to indicate that you now have a wireless network connection.

Simplify It

How do I disconnect from my wireless network?

To disconnect from the network, follow these steps:

① Click the **Network** icon (▥).

② Click your network.

③ Click **Disconnect**.

Windows 7 disconnects from the wireless network.

Chapter 8

Surfing the World Wide Web

After you have your Internet connection up and running, you can use Windows 7's Internet Explorer program to navigate — or **surf** — the sites of the World Wide Web. This chapter explains the Web and shows you how to navigate from site to site by selecting links and entering Web page addresses. You also learn how to open pages in tabs and return to pages you visited previously.

This chapter also shows you how to change your home page, save your favorite pages for easier access later, and search for information on the Web.

Understanding the World Wide Web

The World Wide Web — the Web, for short — is a massive storehouse of information that resides on computers, called *Web servers,* located all over the world.

Each Web server hosts one or more Web sites, and each of those sites contains dozens, hundreds, or even thousands of documents called *pages.*

You navigate from site to site and from page to page by clicking special words, phrases, or images called *links,* or by entering the address of the site or page you want to view. You do all of this using a special software program called a *Web browser.*

Web Page

World Wide Web information is presented on Web pages, which you download to your computer using a Web browser program, such as Windows 7's Internet Explorer. Each Web page can combine text with images, sounds, music, and even video to present you with information on a particular subject. The Web consists of billions of pages covering almost every imaginable topic.

Web Site

A Web site is a collection of Web pages associated with a particular person, business, government, school, or organization. Web sites are stored on a Web server, a special computer that makes Web pages available for people to browse.

Web Address

Every Web page has its own Web address that uniquely identifies the page. This address is sometimes called a *URL* (pronounced *yoo-ar-ell* or *erl*), which is short for Uniform Resource Locator. If you know the address of a page, you can plug that address into your Web browser to view the page.

Links

A *link* (also called a hyperlink) is a kind of "cross-reference" to another Web page. Each link is a bit of text (usually shown underlined and in a different color) or an image that, when you click it, loads the other page into your Web browser automatically. The other page is often from the same site, but it is common to come across links that take you to pages anywhere on the Web.

Start Internet Explorer

You can use Internet Explorer, Windows 7's built-in Web browser program, to surf the Web. To do this, you must first start Internet Explorer.

When you have completed your work on the Web, you should shut down Internet Explorer to reduce clutter on your screen and recover some system resources.

Some versions of Windows 7, particularly those sold in the European Union, do not include the Internet Explorer Web browser. To obtain Internet Explorer, contact your computer manufacturer or Microsoft.

Start Internet Explorer

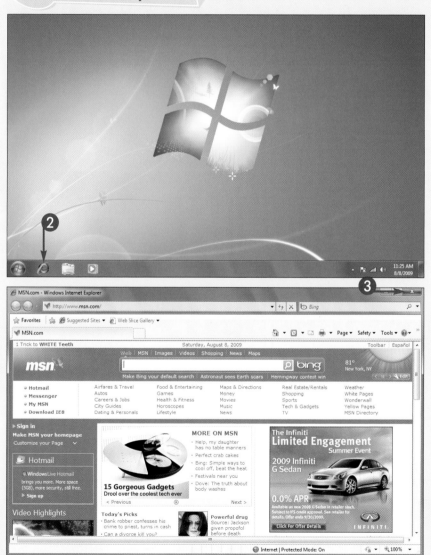

① Connect to the Internet.

② Click **Internet Explorer**.

Note: *If you do not see the Internet Explorer icon in the taskbar, click* **Start**, *click* **All Programs**, *and then click* **Internet Explorer**.

The Internet Explorer window appears.

Note: *If you see the Welcome to Internet Explorer 8 dialog box, click* **Next**, *click* **Use express settings** (○ *changes to* ◉), *and then click* **Finish**.

③ When you are finished with the Web, click the **Close** button (⊠) to shut down Internet Explorer.

Navigate Internet Explorer

If your computer is running Windows, then your default Web browser is most likely Internet Explorer. This is Microsoft's browser, and it comes with most versions of Windows, which is part of the reason why it is the most popular browser in use today.

This section introduces you to the main features of the Internet Explorer window. You can more easily surf the Web if you know your way around the Internet Explorer Web browser.

Web Page Title

This part of the Internet Explorer title bar displays the title of the displayed Web page.

Address Bar

This text box displays the address of the displayed Web page. You can also use the address bar to type the address of a Web page that you want to visit.

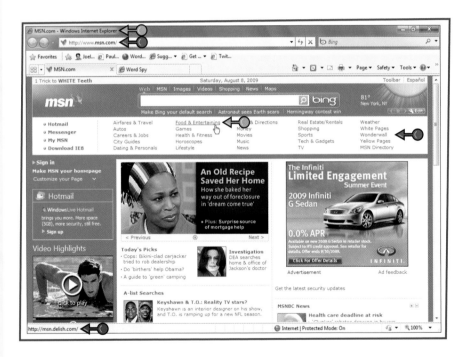

Links

Links appear either as text or as images. On most pages (although not the page shown here), text links appear underlined and in a different color (usually blue) than the regular page text.

Current Link

This is the link that you are currently pointing at with your mouse. The mouse pointer changes from ⬚ to 🖑. On some pages, the link text also becomes underlined (as shown here) and changes color.

Status Bar

This area displays the current status of Internet Explorer. For example, it displays "Opening page" when you are downloading a Web page, and "Done" when the page is fully loaded. When you point at a link, the status bar displays the address of the page associated with the link.

Select a Link

Almost all Web pages include links to other pages that contain information related to something in the current page, and you can use these links to navigate to other Web pages. When you select a link, your Web browser loads the other page.

Knowing what words, phrases, or images are links is not always obvious. The only way to tell for sure in many cases is to position the ⌖ over the text or image; if the ⌖ changes to a ⌐, you know you are dealing with a link.

Select a Link

❶ Position the ⌖ over the link (⌖ changes to ⌐).

❷ Click the text or image.

● The status bar shows the current download status.

Note: *The address shown in the status bar when you point at a link may be different from the one shown when the page is downloading. This happens when the Web site "redirects" the link, which happens frequently.*

The linked Web page appears.

● The Web page title and address change after the linked page is loaded.

● The status bar shows Done when the page is completely loaded.

Enter a Web Page Address

If you know the address of a specific Web page, you can type that address into the Web browser and the program will display the page.

Internet Explorer's Address bar also doubles as a list of the Web page addresses you have entered most recently. By pulling down that list you can see these recent addresses and select one to return to that site.

TYPE A WEB PAGE ADDRESS

① Click in the address bar.

② Type the address of the Web page.

③ Click the **Go** button (⬛) or press **Enter**.

The Web page appears.

● The Web page title changes after the page is loaded.

REDISPLAY A WEB PAGE

❶ Click ⊡ in the address bar.

A list of the addresses you have typed appears.

❷ Click the address you want to display.

The Web page appears.

Note: *If you type the first few letters of the address (such as* ***goog***), *the address bar displays a list of addresses that match what you have typed. If you see the address you want, click it to load the page.*

Are there any shortcuts I can use to enter Web page addresses?

Here are some useful keyboard techniques:

● After you finish typing the address, press `Enter` instead of clicking →.

● Most Web addresses begin with *http://*. You can leave off these characters when you type your address; Internet Explorer adds them automatically.

● If the address uses the form http://www.something. com, type just the "something" part and press `Ctrl` + `Enter`. Internet Explorer automatically adds *http://www.* at the beginning and *.com* at the end.

When I try to load a page, why does Internet Explorer tell me "The page cannot be displayed"?

This message means that Internet Explorer is unable to contact a Web server at the address you typed. This is often a temporary glitch, so click **Refresh** (↻) to try loading the page again. If the trouble persists, double-check your address to ensure that you typed it correctly. If you did, the site may be unavailable for some reason. Try again in a few hours.

Open a Web Page in a Tab

You can make it easier to work with multiple Web pages simultaneously by opening each page in its own tab.

When you use a Web browser normally, each page appears in the main part of the browser window, which is usually called the content area. A tab is like a second content area, and it appears "behind" the first one, with only a small tab (hence the name) visible. Click the tab and you see the second content area and its loaded Web page.

You can open as many pages as you want in their own tabs. This is convenient because all the pages appear within a single Internet Explorer window.

Open a Web Page in a Tab

OPEN A WEB PAGE IN A TAB

1 Right-click the link you want to open.

2 Click **Open in New Tab**.

● A new tab appears with the page title.

3 Click the tab to display the page.

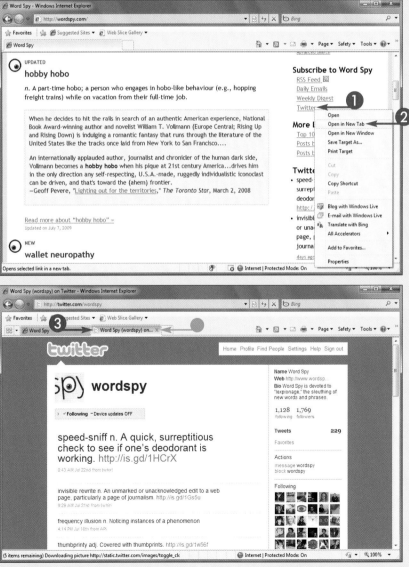

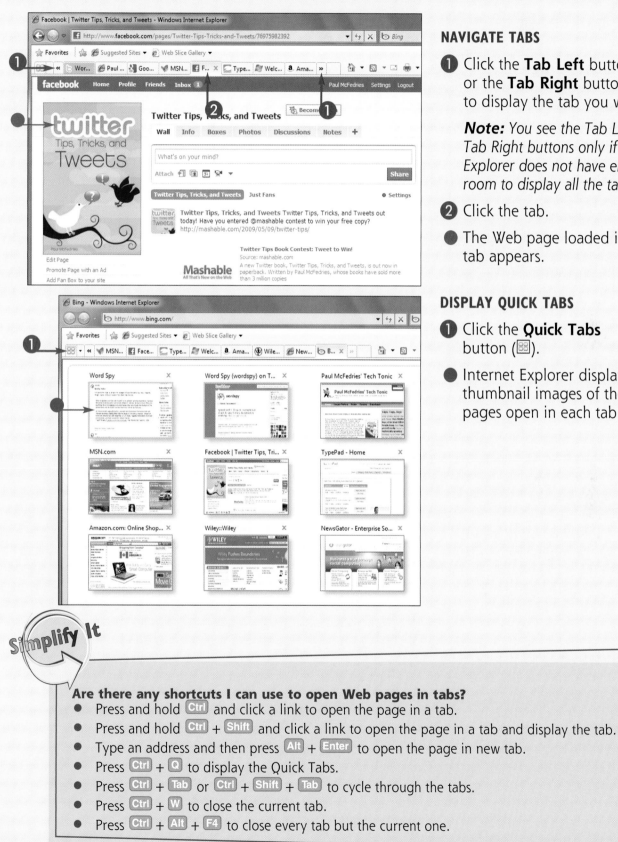

NAVIGATE TABS

1 Click the **Tab Left** button (⊞) or the **Tab Right** button (⊞) to display the tab you want.

Note: You see the Tab Left and Tab Right buttons only if Internet Explorer does not have enough room to display all the tabs.

2 Click the tab.

● The Web page loaded in the tab appears.

DISPLAY QUICK TABS

1 Click the **Quick Tabs** button (⊞).

● Internet Explorer displays thumbnail images of the Web pages open in each tab.

Simplify It

Are there any shortcuts I can use to open Web pages in tabs?
● Press and hold `Ctrl` and click a link to open the page in a tab.
● Press and hold `Ctrl` + `Shift` and click a link to open the page in a tab and display the tab.
● Type an address and then press `Alt` + `Enter` to open the page in new tab.
● Press `Ctrl` + `Q` to display the Quick Tabs.
● Press `Ctrl` + `Tab` or `Ctrl` + `Shift` + `Tab` to cycle through the tabs.
● Press `Ctrl` + `W` to close the current tab.
● Press `Ctrl` + `Alt` + `F4` to close every tab but the current one.

Navigate Web Pages

After you have visited several pages, you can return to a page you visited earlier. Instead of making you retype the address or look for the link, Internet Explorer gives you some easier methods.

When you navigate Web pages, you can go back to a page you have visited in the current browser session. After you have done that, you can also reverse course and go forward through the pages again.

Navigate Web Pages

GO BACK ONE PAGE

① Click the **Back** button (⬅).

The previous page you visited appears.

GO BACK SEVERAL PAGES

① Click the **Recent Pages** ⬇.

A list of the sites you have visited appears.

● The current site appears with a check mark (☑) beside it.

● Items listed below the current site are ones you visited prior to the current site. When you position the mouse ⬚ over a previous site, Internet Explorer displays the **Go Back** arrow (⬅).

② Click the page you want to display.

The page appears.

GO FORWARD ONE PAGE

1 Click the **Forward** button (➡).

The next page you visited appears.

Note: If you are at the last page viewed up to that point, the Forward button (➡) is not active.

GO FORWARD SEVERAL PAGES

1 Click the **Recent Pages** ⬇.

A list of the sites you have visited appears.

● Items listed above the current site are ones you visited after the current site. When you position the mouse ⬍ over a previous site, Internet Explorer displays the Go Forward arrow (➡).

2 Click the page you want to display.

The page appears.

Simplify It

How do I go back or forward to a page, but also keep the current page on-screen?
You can do this by opening a second Internet Explorer window. Keep the current page in the original window and then use the second window to go back or forward.

1 Press Ctrl + N.

● A new Internet Explorer window appears.

2 Use the techniques described in this section to navigate to the page you want.

Change Your Home Page

Your home page is the Web page that appears when you first start Internet Explorer. The default home page is usually the MSN.com site, but you can change that to any other page you want. For example, many people prefer to open a search engine page at startup.

In the Windows 7 version of Internet Explorer, you can have a single home page or you can have multiple home pages that load in separate tabs each time you start the program.

Change Your Home Page

CHANGE A SINGLE HOME PAGE

1. Display the Web page that you want to use as your home page.

2. Click the **Home** button ⬇.

3. Click **Add or Change Home Page**.

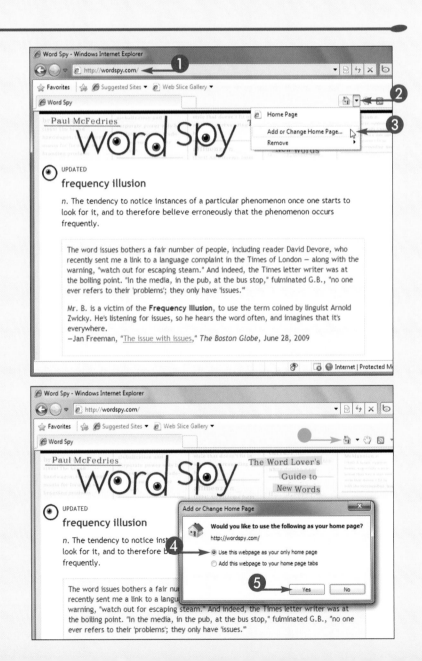

The Add or Change Home Page dialog box appears.

4. Click **Use this webpage as your only home page** (◉ changes to ◉).

5. Click **Yes**.

Internet Explorer changes your home page.

● You can click the **Home** button (🏠) to display the home page at any time.

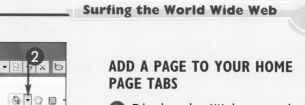

ADD A PAGE TO YOUR HOME PAGE TABS

1. Display the Web page that you want to add to your home page tabs.

2. Click the **Home** button ⊡.

3. Click **Add or Change Home Page**.

The Add or Change Home Page dialog box appears.

4. Click **Add this webpage to your home page tabs** (◎ changes to ◉)

5. Click **Yes**.

Internet Explorer adds the page to your home page tabs.

● You can click the **Home** button (🏠) to display home page tabs at any time.

Note: To return to using your original home page, click **Tools**, click **Internet Options**, click the **General** tab, click **Use default**, and then click **OK**.

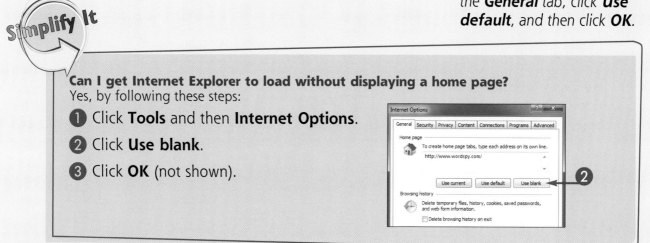

Simplify It

Can I get Internet Explorer to load without displaying a home page?
Yes, by following these steps:

1. Click **Tools** and then **Internet Options**.

2. Click **Use blank**.

3. Click **OK** (not shown).

Save Favorite Web Pages

If you have Web pages that you visit frequently, you can save yourself time by saving those pages as favorites within Internet Explorer. This enables you to display the pages with just a couple of mouse clicks.

The Favorites feature is a list of Web pages that you have saved. Instead of typing an address or searching for one of these pages, you can display the Web page by selecting its address from the Favorites list.

Save Favorite Web Pages

SAVE A FAVORITE WEB PAGE

1 Display the Web page you want to save as a favorite.

2 Click the **Favorites Center** button ( ).

3 Click **Add to Favorites** ( ).

The Add a Favorite dialog box appears.

Note: You can also display the Add a Favorite dialog box by pressing Ctrl + D.

4 Edit the page name, as necessary.

5 Click **Add**.

DISPLAY A FAVORITE WEB PAGE

1 Click the **Favorites Center** button (⭐).

2 Click **Favorites**.

The Favorites list appears.

3 Click the Web page you want to display.

The Web page appears.

● If you use your Favorites list a lot, you can make it easier to display the pages by keeping the Favorites Center visible. Click the **Favorites Center** button (⭐) and then click the **Pin the Favorites Center** button (📌). Internet Explorer pins the Favorites Center to the left side of the window.

Simplify It

How do I delete a favorite?

1 Click the **Favorites Center** button (⭐).

2 Click **Favorites**.

3 Right-click the favorite you want to delete.

4 Click **Delete**.

Internet Explorer asks if you are sure you want to delete the favorite.

5 Click **Yes**.

Search
for Sites

If you need information on a specific topic, Internet Explorer has a built-in Search feature that enables you to quickly search the Web for sites that have the information you require. You type a word or phrase that represents what you are looking for, and Internet Explorer sends the search text to another site that performs the search for you.

The Web has a number of sites called *search engines* that enable you to find what you are looking for. By default, Internet Explorer uses Microsoft's Bing search engine, but you can use other sites.

Search for Sites

① Click in the search box.

② Type a word, phrase, or question that represents the information you want to find.

③ Click the **Search** button ($\wp$) or press Enter.

● A list of pages that match your search text appears.

④ Click a Web page.

The page appears.

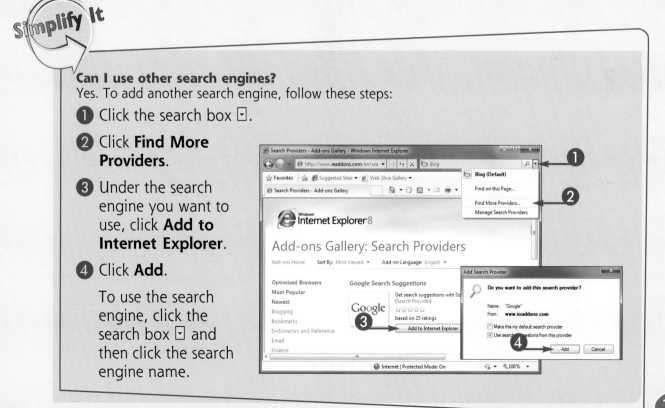

Simplify It

Can I use other search engines?
Yes. To add another search engine, follow these steps:

1 Click the search box ⊡.

2 Click **Find More Providers**.

3 Under the search engine you want to use, click **Add to Internet Explorer**.

4 Click **Add**.

To use the search engine, click the search box ⊡ and then click the search engine name.

Chapter 9

Working with E-mail, Contacts, and Events

You may find that your life is busier than ever, and the number of people you need to stay in touch with, appointments you have to keep, and tasks you have to perform seem to increase daily. Fortunately, you can install the Windows Live Mail program to send e-mail to and read e-mail from friends, family, colleagues, and even total strangers almost anywhere in the world. You can also use

Windows Live Mail's Contacts feature to manage your contacts by storing information such as phone numbers, e-mail addresses, street addresses, and much more. Finally, you use the Calendar feature to enter and track events.

Install Windows Live Essentials Programs

Windows Live Mail is not installed on Windows 7 by default. To use the program, you must access the Windows Live Essentials Web site and then download and install the program from there.

You can also use the Windows Live Essentials site to install other useful programs that do not come with Windows 7, such as Windows Live Photo Gallery and Windows Live Movie Maker.

Install Windows Live Essentials Programs

① Click **Start**.

② Click the **Getting Started** arrow (▶).

③ Click **Get Windows Live Essentials**.

The Windows Live Essentials Web page appears.

④ Click **Download**.

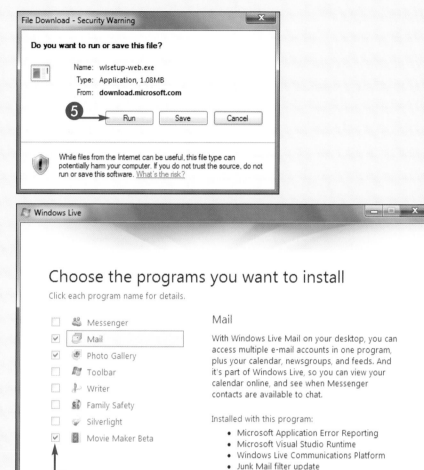

The File Download - Security Warning dialog box appears.

⑤ Click **Run**.

*Note: If you see the User Account Control dialog box at this point, provide an administrator password, if asked for one, and click **Yes**.*

⑥ Click **Close** (⊠) to close the Windows Live Essentials Web page.

The Choose the Programs You Want to Install dialog box appears.

⑦ Click the check box beside each program you want to install (☐ changes to ☑).

⑧ Click **Install**.

Windows 7 installs your selected Windows Live Essentials programs.

Simplify It

Do I have to pay for any Windows Live Essential programs?
No. All of the programs that are available on the Windows Live Essentials Web site, including Windows Live Mail, are free. Microsoft created the Windows Live Essentials programs as supplements to Windows 7, but did not include them in Windows 7 because many people prefer to use other programs, such as Microsoft Outlook for e-mail and contacts.

How do I start a Windows Live Essentials program after it has been installed?
The Windows Live Essentials installation program adds a new submenu named Windows Live to your Start menu. To launch any Windows Live Essential programs, click **Start**, click **All Programs**, and then click **Windows Live**. In the submenu that appears, click the name of the program you want to run, such as **Windows Live Mail**.

Configure an E-mail Account

Before you can send an e-mail message, you must add your e-mail account to the Windows Live Mail application. This also enables you to use Windows Live Mail to retrieve the messages that others have sent to your account.

Your e-mail account is usually a POP (Post Office Protocol) account supplied by your Internet service provider (ISP), which should have supplied you with the POP account details. These details include your e-mail account login user name and password, and possibly the names of the ISP's incoming and outgoing mail servers.

Configure an E-mail Account

① Start Windows Live Mail.

The first time you start the program, the Add an E-mail Account Wizard appears.

Note: *If you are trying to configure a second e-mail account, click the* **Add e-mail account** *link in the Folder pane.*

② Type your e-mail address.

③ Type your e-mail password.

④ Type your name.

⑤ Click **Next**.

Note: *If Windows Live Mail tells you it has successfully set up your account, click* **Finish** *and skip the rest of these steps.*

Windows Live Mail prompts you for your e-mail account's server information.

⑥ Click ⏷ and then click the type of e-mail account.

⑦ Type the name of your ISP's incoming mail server.

⑧ Type the e-mail account login user name.

Add an E-mail Account

Please enter your e-mail account information below:

E-mail address: myname@myisp.com ← ②

example555@hotmail.com   Get a free e-mail account

Password: ●●●●●● ← ③

☑ Remember password

How should your name appear in e-mail sent from this account?

Display Name: Paul McFedries ← ④

For example: John Smith

☐ Manually configure server settings for e-mail account.

⑤ → [Next] [Cancel]

Add an E-mail Account

Where can I find my e-mail server information?

Incoming Server Information

My incoming mail server is a [POP3 ▼] server. ← ⑥

Incoming server: mail.myisp.com ← ⑦   Port: 110

☐ This server requires a secure connection (SSL)

Log on using: [Clear text authentication ▼]

Login ID (if different from e-mail address):

myname ← ⑧

Outgoing Server Information

Outgoing server: Port: 25

☐ This server requires a secure connection (SSL)

☐ My outgoing server requires authentication

[Next] [Cancel]

Add an E-mail Account

Where can I find my e-mail server information?

Incoming Server Information

My incoming mail server is a [POP3 ▼] server.

Incoming server: mail.myisp.com   Port: 110

☐ This server requires a secure connection (SSL)

Log on using: [Clear text authentication   ▼]

Login ID (if different from e-mail address):

myname

Outgoing Server Information

Outgoing server: smtp.myisp.com ◄ **9**   Port: 587 ◄ **10**

☐ This server requires a secure connection (SSL)

11 ► ☑ My outgoing server requires authentication

12 ► [Next]   [Cancel]

Add an E-mail Account

You have successfully entered in the information required to set up your account.

9 Type the name of your ISP's outgoing mail server.

10 If your ISP uses a different port for outgoing mail, type the port number.

11 Click this check box if your ISP's outgoing mail server requires authentication (☐ changes to ☑).

12 Click **Next**.

The final wizard dialog box appears.

13 Click **Finish** at the bottom of dialog box (not shown).

Windows Live Mail configures your e-mail account.

Simplify It

How do I make changes to an e-mail account?
After you configure your e-mail account, Windows Live Mail adds the account to the Folder pane on the left side of the program window. To make changes to the account, right-click the account name and then click **Properties**. In the Properties dialog box that appears, use the tabs to make changes to your settings (●).

My Account Properties

General | Servers | Connection | Security | Advanced ◄

Mail Account

Type the name by which you would like to refer to these servers. For example: "Work" or "Windows Live Hotmail".

My Account

User Information

Name: Paul McFedries

Organization:

E-mail address: myname@myisp.com

Send an E-mail Message

If you know the e-mail address of a person or organization, you can send an e-mail message to that address. In most cases, the message is delivered within a few minutes.

An e-mail address is a set of characters that uniquely identifies the location of an Internet mailbox. Each e-mail address takes the form *username@domain*, where *username* is the

name of the person's account with the ISP or within his or her organization; and *domain* is the Internet name of the company that provides the person's e-mail account.

If you do not know any e-mail addresses, or, if at first, you prefer to just practice sending messages, you can send messages to your own e-mail address.

Send an E-mail Message

1 Click **New**.

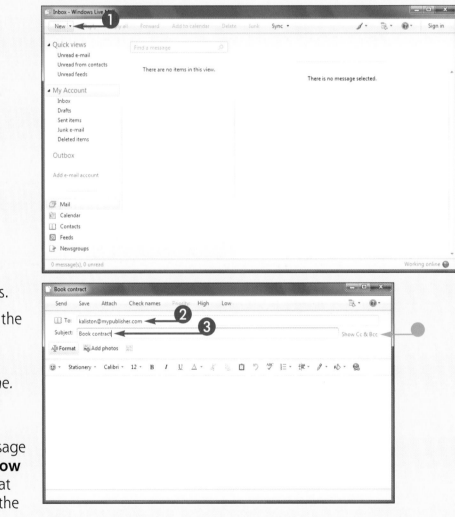

A message window appears.

2 Type the e-mail address of the recipient.

Note: *You can add multiple e-mail addresses to the To line. Separate each address with a semicolon (;).*

● To send a copy of the message to another person, click **Show Cc & Bcc** and then type that person's e-mail address in the **Cc** field that appears.

3 Type a title or short description for the message.

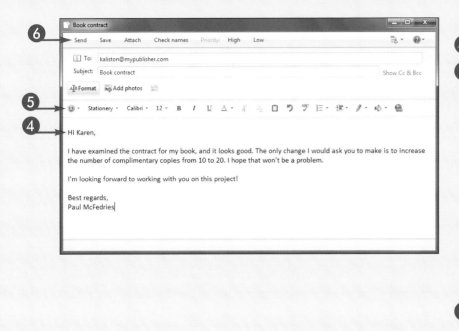

4 Type the message.

5 Use the buttons in the Formatting bar to format the message text.

Note: *Many people use e-mail programs that cannot process text formatting. Unless you are sure your recipient's program supports formatting, it is best to send plain text messages. To do this, press* Alt *, click* **Format***, and then click* **Plain text** *(* ◉ *appears beside the command).*

6 Click **Send**.

Windows Live Mail sends your message.

Note: *Windows Live Mail stores a copy of your message in the Sent Items folder.*

Simplify It

I have a large number of messages to compose. Do I have to be online to do this?
No, composing all the messages while you are offline is possible. Follow these steps:

1 While disconnected from the Internet, start Windows Live Mail, and click **Cancel** if the program asks you to connect to the Internet.

● Windows Live Mail displays Working Offline in the status bar.

2 Compose and send the message. Each time you click **Send**, your messages are stored temporarily in the Outbox folder.

3 After you are done, connect to the Internet.

4 Click **Working Offline**.

Windows Live Mail changes the status bar text to Working Online.

5 Click the **Sync** ▾.

6 Click your e-mail account.

Add Someone to Your Contacts

You can use Windows Live Contacts to store the names and e-mail addresses of people with whom you frequently correspond. You do that by creating a new contact, which is an item called a *card* that stores data about a person or company.

Each card can store a wide variety of information. For example, you can store a person's name, company name, phone numbers, e-mail address and instant messaging data, street address, notes, and much more.

When you choose a name from Windows Live Contacts while composing a message, Windows Live Mail automatically adds the contact's e-mail address. This is faster and more accurate than typing the address by hand.

Add Someone to Your Contacts

1 Click **Contacts** (⊞).

Note: *You can also open Windows Live Contacts by pressing* Ctrl + Shift + C.

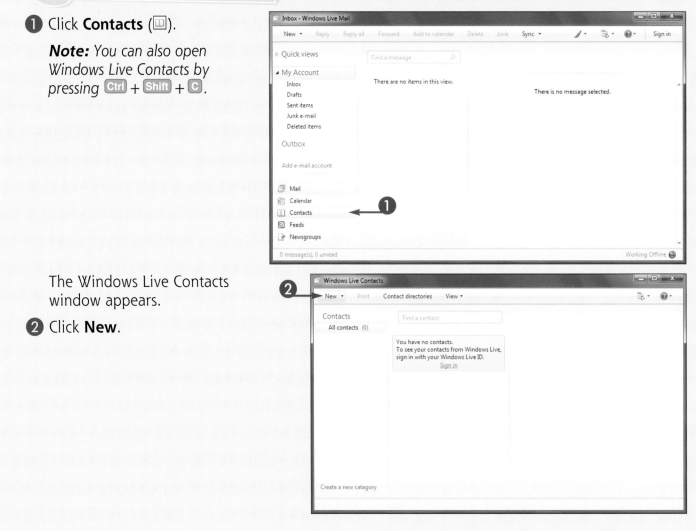

The Windows Live Contacts window appears.

2 Click **New**.

Add a Contact

Quick add
Contact
Personal
Work
IM
Notes
IDs

First name: **3** Paul

Last name: **4** Sellars

Personal e-mail: **5** psellars@logophilia.com

Home phone:

Company:

6 → Add contact   Cancel

Windows Live Contacts

New ▾   Edit   Delete   E-mail   Print   Contact directories   View ▾

Contacts
All contacts (1)

Find a contact

Paul Sellars
psellars@logophilia.com

Paul Sellars

Personal info
Full name   Paul Sellars
Personal e-mail psellars@logophilia.com

Work info
Add contact info

Other info
Add contact info

The Add a Contact dialog box appears.

3 Type the person's first name.

4 Type the person's last name.

5 Type the person's e-mail address.

Note: You can use the other tabs in the Add a Contact dialog box to store more information about the contact, including home and business addresses and phone numbers, spouse name, birthday, and more.

6 Click **Add contact**.

● Windows Live Contacts adds the person to the Contacts list.

Simplify It

How do I edit a person's contact data?
In the Windows Live Contacts window, click the person you want to work with and then click **Edit** in the toolbar. (You can also double-click the person's name or click any of the **Add contact info** links that appear in the contact data section.) Use the Edit Contact dialog box to make your changes, and then click **Save**.

How do I delete someone from my Contacts?
In the Windows Live Contacts window, click the person you want to work with and then click **Delete** in the toolbar. When Windows Live Contacts asks you to confirm the deletion, click **OK**.

Create a Contact Category

You can organize your contacts into one or more categories, which is useful if you want to view just a subset of your contacts. For example, you could create one category for your work colleagues, another for your family members, a third for people working on a current project, and so on.

Categories are particularly handy if you have a large number of contacts in Windows Live Contacts. By creating and maintaining categories, you can navigate your contacts more easily. You can also perform category-wide tasks, such as sending a single e-mail message that gets distributed to everyone in the category.

Create a Contact Category

1 Click the **New** ⊡.

2 Click **Category**.

● You can also click the **Create a new category** link.

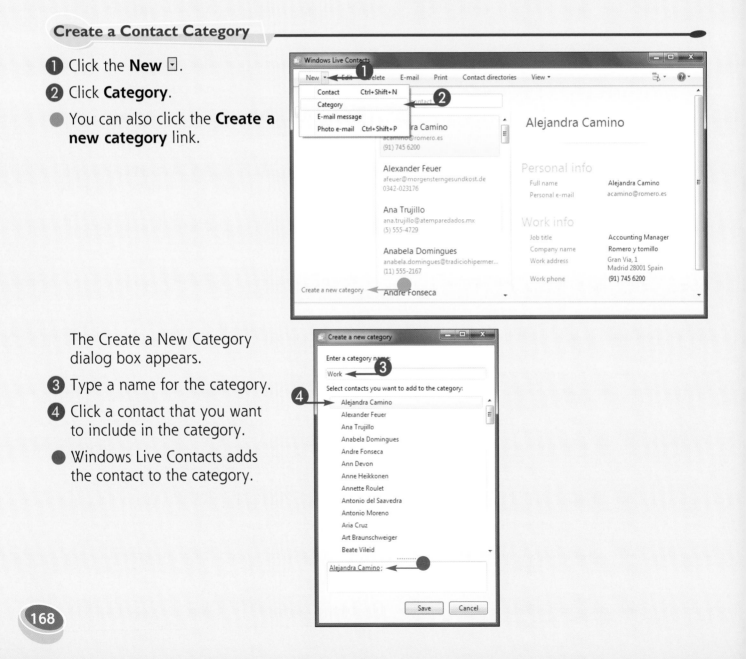

The Create a New Category dialog box appears.

3 Type a name for the category.

4 Click a contact that you want to include in the category.

● Windows Live Contacts adds the contact to the category.

⑤ Repeat Step **4** for the other contacts you want to add to the category.

Note: *If you add the wrong contact by accident, you can remove it by clicking the contact name again.*

⑥ Click **Save**.

● Windows Live Contacts adds the category.

Simplify It

Can I send an e-mail message to all the contacts in a category?
Yes, this is one of the best reasons to create a category. Normally, sending an e-mail message to multiple contacts involves typing or selecting multiple addresses. With a category, however, you send a single message to the category, and Windows Live Mail automatically sends a copy to each member. Right-click the category and then click **Send e-mail**.

How do I edit or delete a category?
If you want to add new contacts to the category or delete existing contacts, right-click the category and then click **Edit Category** (or double-click the category). If you want to delete a category, right-click the category and then click **Delete Category**. When Windows Live Contacts asks you to confirm the deletion, click **OK**.

Select a Contact Address

After you have some e-mail addresses and names in your Windows Live Contacts list, when composing a message, you can select the address you want directly from Windows Live Contacts instead of typing the address. This is much faster and more accurate than typing the address by hand, particularly if you are sending the message to multiple people.

Select a Contact Address

① In Windows Live Mail, click **New** to start a new message.

② Click **To**.

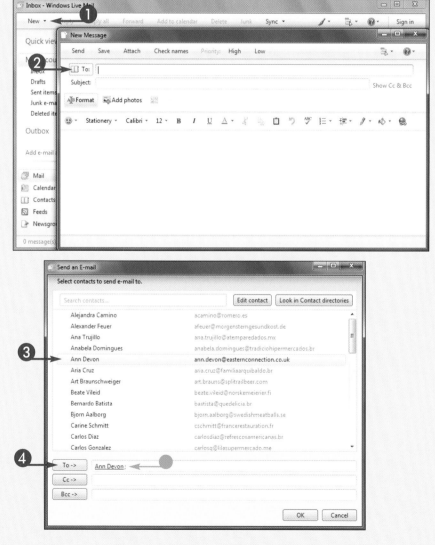

The Send an E-mail dialog box appears.

③ Click the person to whom you want to send the message.

④ Click **To**.

● The person's name appears in the To box.

Note: *You can also double-click a contact to add that person to the To field.*

⑤ Repeat Steps **3** and **4** to add other recipients to the To box.

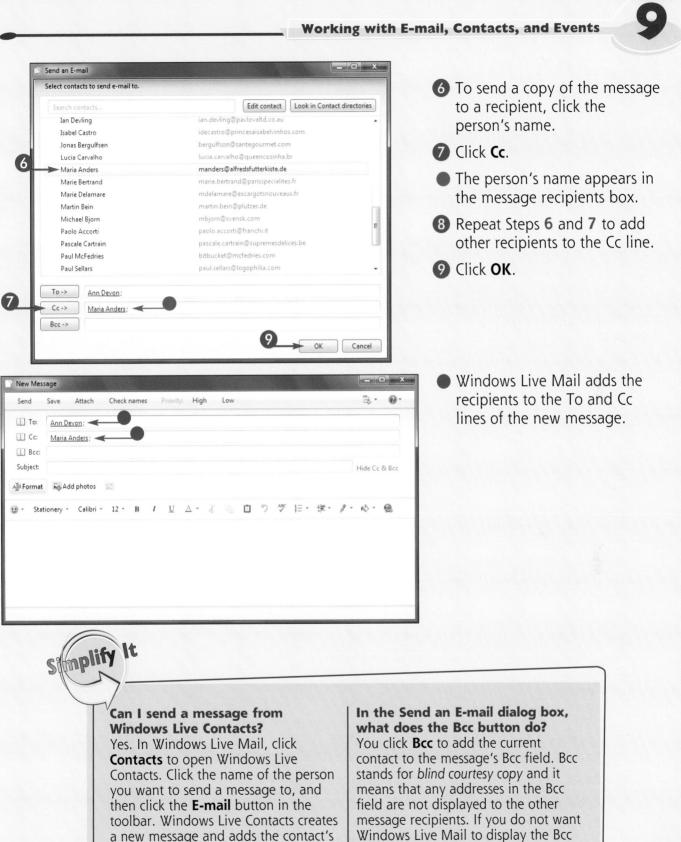

6 To send a copy of the message to a recipient, click the person's name.

7 Click **Cc**.

● The person's name appears in the message recipients box.

8 Repeat Steps **6** and **7** to add other recipients to the Cc line.

9 Click **OK**.

● Windows Live Mail adds the recipients to the To and Cc lines of the new message.

Simplify It

Can I send a message from Windows Live Contacts?
Yes. In Windows Live Mail, click **Contacts** to open Windows Live Contacts. Click the name of the person you want to send a message to, and then click the **E-mail** button in the toolbar. Windows Live Contacts creates a new message and adds the contact's name to the To field automatically.

In the Send an E-mail dialog box, what does the Bcc button do?
You click **Bcc** to add the current contact to the message's Bcc field. Bcc stands for *blind courtesy copy* and it means that any addresses in the Bcc field are not displayed to the other message recipients. If you do not want Windows Live Mail to display the Bcc field in the message window, click **Hide Cc & Bcc**.

Add a File Attachment

If you have a memo, an image, or another document that you want to send to another person, you can attach the document to an e-mail message. The other person can then open the document after he or she receives your message.

You might find that you need to send someone something more complex than a simple text e-mail, such as budget numbers, a slide show,

or some form of media that you want to share, such as an image or a song.

Because these more complex types of data usually come in a separate file — such as a spreadsheet, a presentation file, a picture file, or a music file — it makes sense to send that file to your recipient. You do this in e-mail by attaching the file to a message.

Add a File Attachment

ADD AN ATTACHMENT FROM A DIALOG BOX

1. Click **New** to start a new message.

2. Click **Attach**.

The Open dialog box appears.

3. Click the file you want to attach.

4. Click **Open**.

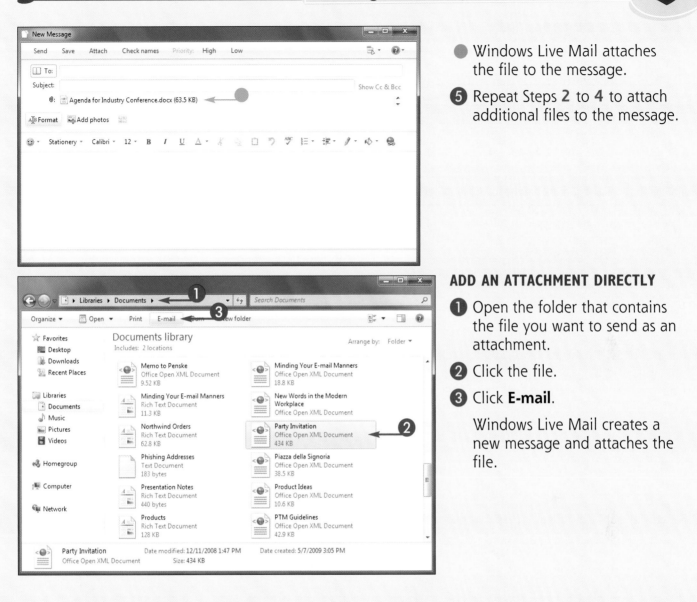

● Windows Live Mail attaches the file to the message.

❺ Repeat Steps **2** to **4** to attach additional files to the message.

ADD AN ATTACHMENT DIRECTLY

❶ Open the folder that contains the file you want to send as an attachment.

❷ Click the file.

❸ Click **E-mail**.

Windows Live Mail creates a new message and attaches the file.

Simplify It

Is there a limit to the number of files I can attach to a message?
There is no practical limit to the number of files you can attach to the message. However, you should be careful with the total *size* of the files you send. If you or the recipient has a slow Internet connection, sending or receiving the message can take an extremely long time. Also, many Internet service providers (ISPs) place a limit on the size of a message's attachments, which is usually between 2MB and 10MB. In general, use e-mail to send only a few small files at a time.

Add a Signature

In an e-mail message, a *signature* is a small amount of text that appears at the bottom of the message. Instead of typing this information manually, you can create the signature once and then have Windows Live Mail add the signature automatically to any message you send.

Signatures usually contain personal contact information, such as your phone numbers,

business address, and e-mail and Web site addresses. Some people supplement their signatures with wise or witty quotations.

Windows Live Mail also supports multiple signatures, which is useful if you use Mail for different purposes such as business and personal. You can also configure Mail to automatically add one of your signatures to any message you send.

Add a Signature

ADD A SIGNATURE

❶ Click **Menus** (📑).

❷ Click **Options**.

The Options dialog box appears.

❸ Click the **Signatures** tab.

❹ Click **New**.

● Windows Live Mail adds a new signature.

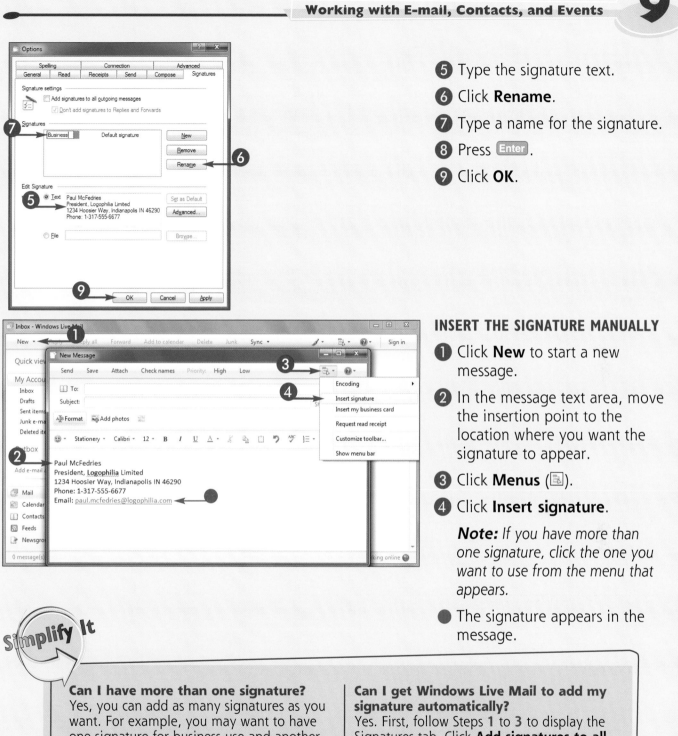

5 Type the signature text.

6 Click **Rename**.

7 Type a name for the signature.

8 Press Enter.

9 Click **OK**.

INSERT THE SIGNATURE MANUALLY

1 Click **New** to start a new message.

2 In the message text area, move the insertion point to the location where you want the signature to appear.

3 Click **Menus** (🔲).

4 Click **Insert signature**.

Note: If you have more than one signature, click the one you want to use from the menu that appears.

● The signature appears in the message.

Can I have more than one signature?
Yes, you can add as many signatures as you want. For example, you may want to have one signature for business use and another for personal use. To add multiple signatures, follow Steps **1** to **3** to display the Signatures tab, and then follow Steps **4** to **8** for each signature. Be sure to give each signature a descriptive name.

Can I get Windows Live Mail to add my signature automatically?
Yes. First, follow Steps **1** to **3** to display the Signatures tab. Click **Add signatures to all outgoing messages** (☐ changes to ☑) to have Windows Live Mail add your signature to the bottom of every new message. Click **Don't add signatures to Replies and Forwards** (☑ changes to ☐) if you want Windows Live Mail to add your signature when you reply to and forward messages.

Receive and Read E-mail Messages

You must connect to your mail provider's incoming mail server to retrieve and read messages sent to you.

When another person sends you an e-mail message, that message ends up in your e-mail account's mailbox on the incoming mail server your **ISP** or e-mail provider maintains. However, that company does not automatically pass along that message to you. Instead, you must use Mail to connect to your mailbox on the incoming mail server and then retrieve any messages waiting for you.

By default, Windows Live Mail checks for new messages automatically when you start the program, and then checks for more messages every 30 minutes while you are online.

Receive and Read E-mail Messages

RECEIVE E-MAIL MESSAGES

1 Click **Inbox**.

2 Click **Sync**.

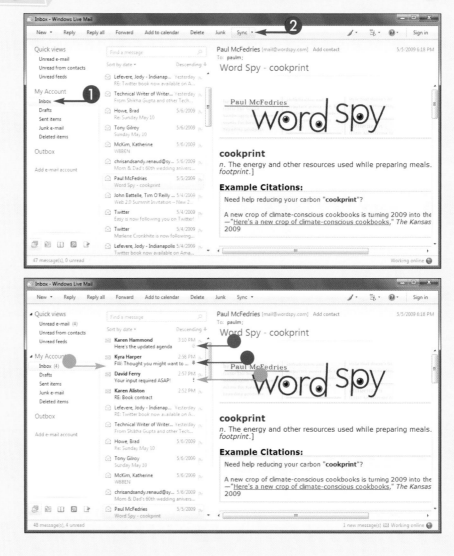

● If you have new messages, they appear in your Inbox folder in bold type.

● This symbol (⬚) means that the message came with a file attached.

● This symbol (⬚) means the message was sent as low priority.

● This symbol (⬚) means the message was sent as high priority.

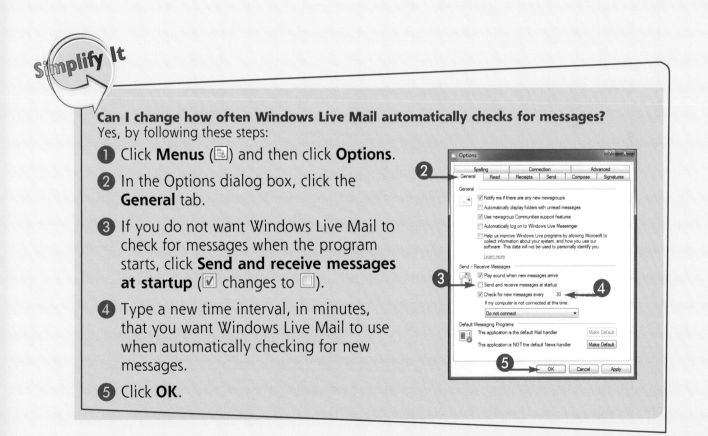

READ A MESSAGE

1 Click the message.

2 Read the message text in the preview pane.

Note: *If you want to open the message in its own window, double-click the message.*

Simplify It

Can I change how often Windows Live Mail automatically checks for messages?
Yes, by following these steps:

1 Click **Menus** (⊟) and then click **Options**.

2 In the Options dialog box, click the **General** tab.

3 If you do not want Windows Live Mail to check for messages when the program starts, click **Send and receive messages at startup** (☑ changes to ☐).

4 Type a new time interval, in minutes, that you want Windows Live Mail to use when automatically checking for new messages.

5 Click **OK**.

Reply to a Message

When a message you receive requires some kind of response — whether it is answering a question, supplying information, or providing comments or criticisms — you can reply to any message you receive.

Most replies go only to the person who sent the original message. However, it is also possible to send the reply to all the people who were included in the original message's To line and Cc line.

When it creates the reply message, Windows Live Mail automatically adds "Re:" to the beginning of the subject line to indicate the message is a reply.

Windows Live Mail also includes the text of the original message in the reply, but you should edit the original message text to include only enough of the original message to put your reply into context.

Reply to a Message

1 Click the message to which you want to reply.

2 Click the reply type you want to use:

Click **Reply** to respond only to the first address displayed on the From line.

Click **Reply All** to respond to all the addresses in the From and Cc lines.

A message window appears.

● Windows Live Mail automatically inserts the recipient addresses.

● Windows Live Mail also inserts the subject line, preceded by Re.

● Windows Live Mail includes the original message's addresses (To and From), date, subject, and text at the bottom of the reply.

Re: Article idea

Send Save Attach Check names Priority: High Low

To: Andrea Aster;

Subject: Re: Article idea   Show Cc & Bcc

From: "Andrea Aster"
Sent: Friday, May 08, 2009 3:34 PM
To: "'Paul McFedries'"
Subject: Article idea

> Hi Paul,
>
> As you know, Twitter is really big right now, so I would like to commission
> an article that explores how writers are using Twitter to connect with their   **3**
> readers and promote their books. Is this something you would be interested
> in writing? I am thinking it would be about 1,000 words.

Re: Article idea

Send **5** Save Attach Check names Priority: High Low

To: Andrea Aster;

Subject: Re: Article idea   Show Cc & Bcc

Hi Andrea,

Your article idea is great, and so timely! I am definitely interested in writing the piece. When   **4**
do you need it?

---

3 Edit the original message to include only the text relevant to your reply.

Note: *If the original message is fairly short, you usually do not need to edit the text. However, if the original message is long, and your response deals only with part of that message, you will save the recipient time by deleting everything except the relevant portion of the text.*

4 Click the area above the original message text and type your reply.

5 Click **Send**.

Windows Live Mail sends your reply.

Note: *Windows Live Mail stores a copy of your reply in the Sent Items folder.*

Simplify It

After I reply to a message, Windows Live Mail sometimes adds the recipient to my Contacts list. How do I prevent this?
By default, Windows Live Mail adds a person to your Contacts list after the third time you send that person a reply. To turn this off, follow these steps:

1 Click **Menus** (🗐) and click **Options**.

2 In the Options dialog box, click the **Send** tab.

3 Click **Automatically put people I reply to in my address book after the third reply** (☑ changes to ☐).

4 Click **OK** (not shown).

Forward a Message

If a message has information relevant to or that concerns another person, you can forward a copy of that message to the other recipient. You can also include your own comments in the forward.

When it creates the forward message, Windows Live Mail automatically adds "Fw:" to the beginning of the subject line to indicate the message is a forward.

In the body of the forward, Mail also includes the original message's addresses, date, and subject line.

Below this information Windows Live Mail also includes the text of the original message. In most cases you will leave the entire message intact so your recipient can see it. However, if only part of the message is relevant to the recipient, you should edit the original message accordingly.

Forward a Message

① Click the message that you want to forward.

② Click **Forward**.

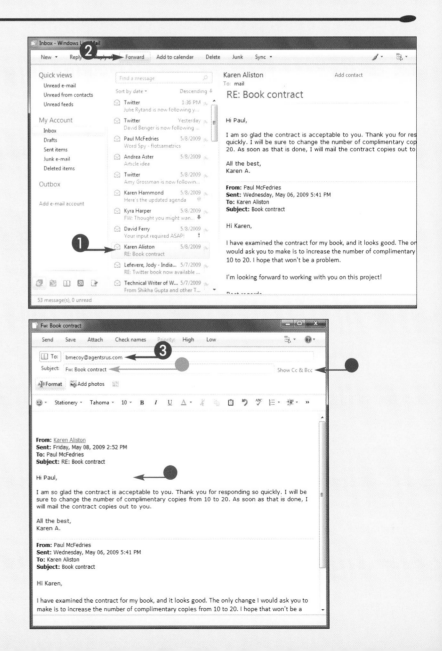

A message window appears.

● Windows Live Mail inserts the subject line, preceded by Fw.

● The original message's addresses (To and From), date, subject, and text are included at the bottom of the forward.

③ Type the e-mail address of the person to whom you are forwarding the message.

● To send a copy of the message to another person, click **Show Cc & Bcc** and then type that person's e-mail address in the **Cc** field that appears.

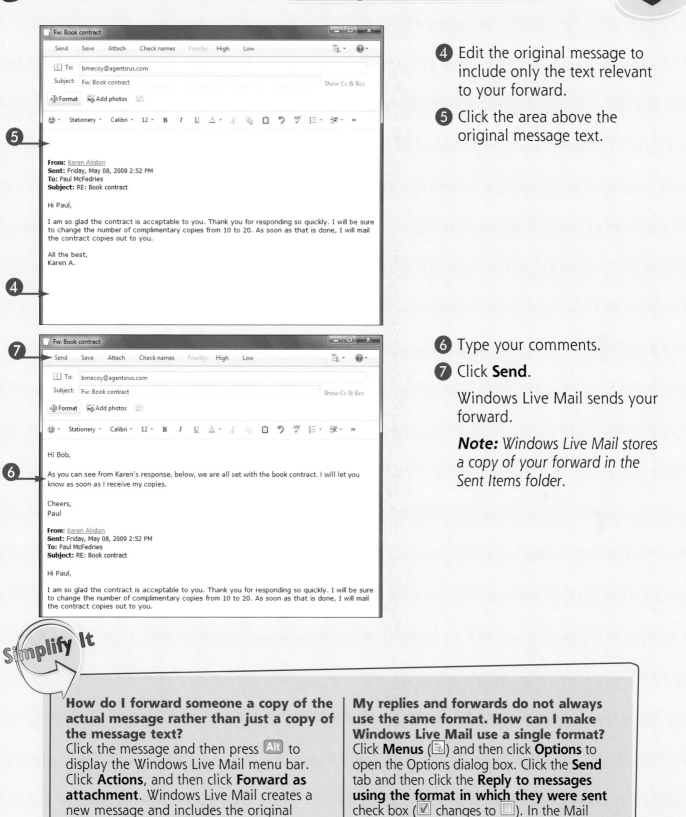

④ Edit the original message to include only the text relevant to your forward.

⑤ Click the area above the original message text.

⑥ Type your comments.

⑦ Click **Send**.

Windows Live Mail sends your forward.

Note: *Windows Live Mail stores a copy of your forward in the Sent Items folder.*

How do I forward someone a copy of the actual message rather than just a copy of the message text?
Click the message and then press Alt to display the Windows Live Mail menu bar. Click **Actions**, and then click **Forward as attachment**. Windows Live Mail creates a new message and includes the original message as an attachment.

My replies and forwards do not always use the same format. How can I make Windows Live Mail use a single format?
Click **Menus** (🗐) and then click **Options** to open the Options dialog box. Click the **Send** tab and then click the **Reply to messages using the format in which they were sent** check box (☑ changes to ☐). In the Mail Sending Format area, click the format you want to use (○ changes to ◉) and then click **OK**.

Open and Save an Attachment

If you receive an e-mail message that has a file attached, you can open the attachment to view the contents of the file. You can also save the attachment as a file on your computer.

Be careful when dealing with attached files. Computer viruses are often transmitted by e-mail attachments. If you do not know the person who sent you the file, do not open it. If the message came from someone you know and you were expecting the file, then it should be safe to open the file; if you were not expecting the file, however, you should write back to have the person confirm that the file is legitimate.

Open and Save an Attachment

OPEN AN ATTACHMENT

1 Click the message that has the attachment, as indicated by the **Attachment** symbol (⬚).

● A list of the message attachments appears.

2 Double-click the attachment you want to open.

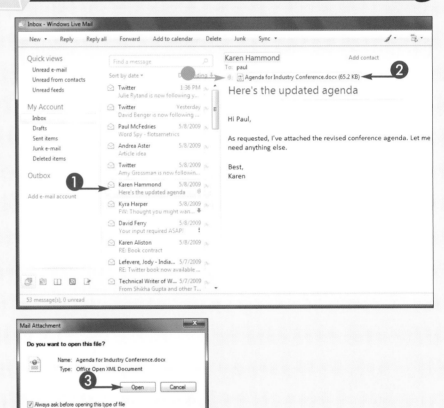

Windows Live Mail asks you to confirm that you want to open the file.

3 Click **Open**.

The file opens in the appropriate program.

Note: *Instead of opening the file, Windows 7 may display a dialog box saying that the file "does not have a program associated with it." This means you need to install the appropriate program for the type of file. If you are not sure, ask the person who sent you the file what program you need.*

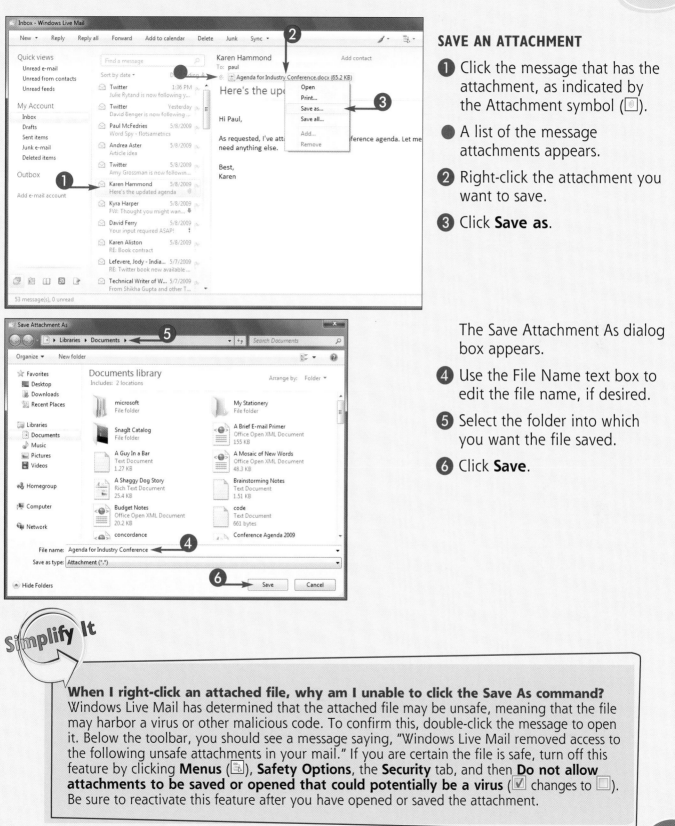

SAVE AN ATTACHMENT

① Click the message that has the attachment, as indicated by the Attachment symbol (📎).

● A list of the message attachments appears.

② Right-click the attachment you want to save.

③ Click **Save as**.

The Save Attachment As dialog box appears.

④ Use the File Name text box to edit the file name, if desired.

⑤ Select the folder into which you want the file saved.

⑥ Click **Save**.

When I right-click an attached file, why am I unable to click the Save As command?
Windows Live Mail has determined that the attached file may be unsafe, meaning that the file may harbor a virus or other malicious code. To confirm this, double-click the message to open it. Below the toolbar, you should see a message saying, "Windows Live Mail removed access to the following unsafe attachments in your mail." If you are certain the file is safe, turn off this feature by clicking **Menus** (📄), **Safety Options**, the **Security** tab, and then **Do not allow attachments to be saved or opened that could potentially be a virus** (☑ changes to ☐). Be sure to reactivate this feature after you have opened or saved the attachment.

Switch to Calendar

With Calendar, the scheduling program that comes with Windows Live Mail, you can create and work with *events*, which are either scheduled appointments such as meetings, lunches, and visits to the dentist, or all-day activities, such as conferences or vacations. The Calendar feature also enables you to create recurring events that automatically repeat at the interval you specify. To get started, you must first switch to the Calendar feature.

Switch to Calendar

① Click **Calendar** (📅).

> **Note:** You can also open the Calendar by pressing
> Ctrl + Shift + X .

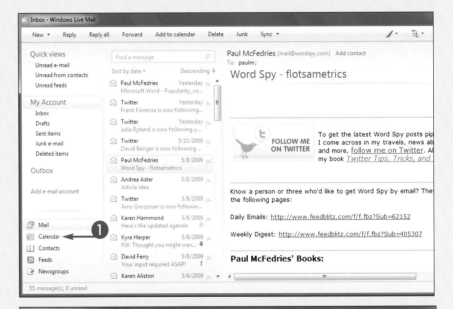

The Calendar window appears.

② When you finish your scheduling chores, click the **Mail** button (📧), or press Ctrl + Shift + J , to return to the Mail feature.

Navigate the Calendar

Windows Live Mail's Calendar makes scheduling easy. However, you can make it even easier by taking some time now to learn the layout of the Calendar window. The most important features are the Date Navigator, the current date display, the event list, and the Calendars list.

Date Navigator

This area shows the current month, and you use the Date Navigator to select the date on which you want to schedule an event, all-day event, or task. See the "Display a Different Date" section, later in this chapter, to learn how to use the Date Navigator.

Current Date

This area shows the date that is currently selected in the Date Navigator.

Calendars

This area shows a list of your calendars. You get a single calendar to start with, but you can add more calendars as described in the "Add a Calendar" section, later in this chapter.

Event List

This area shows the events that you have scheduled. In Day view, as shown here, the event list is divided into half-hour increments.

Display a Different Date

Before you add an event to your calendar, you must first select the date when the event occurs. You use the Date Navigator to display a different date in Calendar and you can navigate dates by month or by year.

Calendar also lets you change the calendar view to suit your needs. For example, you can show just a single day's worth of appointments if you want to concentrate on that day's activities. Similarly, you can view a week's worth of appointments if you want to get a larger sense of what your overall schedule looks like.

Display a Different Date

NAVIGATE BY MONTH

1 In the Date Navigator, click the **Next Month** button (▶) until the month of your event appears.

● If you go too far, click the **Previous Month** button (◀) to move back to the month you want.

2 Click the date.

● The date appears in the events list.

● If you want to return to today's date, click **Go to today**.

NAVIGATE BY YEAR

1 In the Date Navigator, click the month.

Calendar switches to Year view.

2 Click the **Next Year** button (▶) until the year of your event appears.

● If you go too far, click the **Previous Year** button (◀) to move back to the year you want.

3 Click the month when your event occurs.

Calendar switches back to Month view.

4 Use Steps **1** and **2** on the previous page to display and select the date when your event occurs.

Simplify It

Can I see more than one day at a time in the events list?
Yes. Use the following toolbar button to select the view you want to use:

● **Day**. Shows the date currently selected in the Date Navigator. (You can also press Ctrl + Alt + 1.)

● **Week**. Shows the full week that includes the date currently selected in the Date Navigator. (You can also press Ctrl + Alt + 2.)

● **Month**. Shows the month that includes the date currently selected in the Date Navigator. (You can also press Ctrl + Alt + 3.)

Create an Event

You can help organize your life by using Windows Live Mail's Calendar to record your events on the date and time they occur.

If the event has a set time and duration — for example, a meeting or a lunch date — you add the event directly to the calendar as a regular appointment.

If the event has no set time — for example, a birthday, anniversary, or multiple-day event

such as a sales meeting or vacation — you can create an all-day event.

If you have an activity or appointment that recurs at a regular interval, you can create an event and configure it to automatically repeat in Calendar. This saves you from having to repeatedly add the future events yourself because Calendar adds them for you automatically.

Create an Event

① Navigate to the date when the event occurs.

② Click the time when the event starts.

> **Note:** If the event is more than half an hour, you can also click and drag the mouse ⇩ over the full event period.

③ Click **New**.

> **Note:** Another way to start a new event is to press `Ctrl` + `Shift` + `E`.

Calendar displays the New Event dialog box.

④ Type a name for the event.

⑤ Use the Location text box to type the event location.

⑥ If the event is an anniversary or other event that lasts all day, click **All day** (☐ changes to ☑).

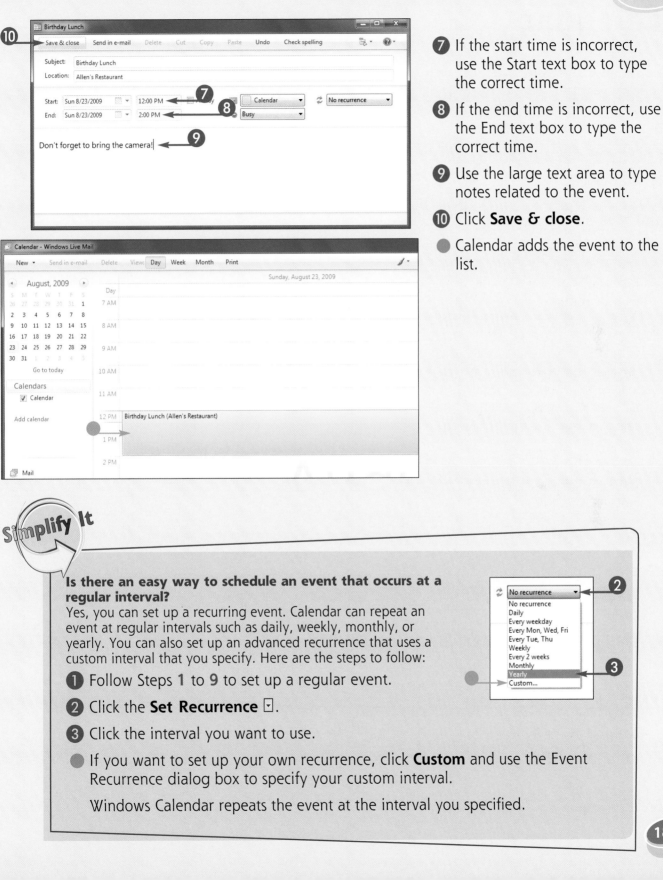

7 If the start time is incorrect, use the Start text box to type the correct time.

8 If the end time is incorrect, use the End text box to type the correct time.

9 Use the large text area to type notes related to the event.

10 Click **Save & close**.

● Calendar adds the event to the list.

Simplify It

Is there an easy way to schedule an event that occurs at a regular interval?
Yes, you can set up a recurring event. Calendar can repeat an event at regular intervals such as daily, weekly, monthly, or yearly. You can also set up an advanced recurrence that uses a custom interval that you specify. Here are the steps to follow:

1 Follow Steps **1** to **9** to set up a regular event.

2 Click the **Set Recurrence** ☑.

3 Click the interval you want to use.

● If you want to set up your own recurrence, click **Custom** and use the Event Recurrence dialog box to specify your custom interval.

Windows Calendar repeats the event at the interval you specified.

Add a Calendar

If you have different schedules that you want to keep separate, you can add another calendar. For example, you might want to have one calendar for work events and a second calendar for personal events. You could also set up different calendars for individual people, different projects, separate clients, and so on.

You can assign different colors to each calendar, which helps you to see at a glance which event belongs to which calendar.

Add a Calendar

1 Click **Add calendar**.

Note: *Another way to start a new calendar is to press* Ctrl + Shift + D.

The Add a Calendar dialog box appears.

2 Type a name for the calendar.

3 Click the color you want to use for the calendar.

④ Type an optional description for the calendar.

⑤ If you want Windows Live Mail to use this calendar as the default for new events, click **Make this my primary calendar** (☐ changes to ☑).

⑥ Click **Save**.

● The new calendar appears in the Calendars list.

How do I assign an event to a particular calendar?
For new events, click the calendar you want to use, and then click **New event** in the menu that appears. You can also click **New** to open the New Event window, click the **Calendar** ⏷, and then click the calendar you want to use. For existing events, double-click the event, click the **Calendar** ⏷, and then click the calendar.

Can I rename the original calendar?
Yes. The default name of "Calendar" is not very descriptive, so it is a good idea to rename it to something more useful. In the Calendars list, click **Calendar** and then click **Properties** in the menu that appears. Use the **Calendar name** text box to type a new name, and then click **Save**.

Chapter 10

Implementing Security in Windows 7

Threats to your computer-related security and privacy often come from the Internet in the form of system intruders, such as junk e-mail, viruses, and identity thieves. However, many security and privacy violations occur right at your computer by someone simply using your computer while you are not around. To protect yourself and your family, you need to understand these threats and know what you can do to thwart them.

This chapter gives you some background information about security in Windows 7, and then shows you various methods for securing your computer.

Understanding Windows 7 Security

Before getting to the details of securing your PC, it helps to take a step back and look at the security and privacy tools that Windows 7 makes available.

These tools include your user account password, Windows 7's User Account Control and Parental Controls features, the Windows Firewall, the Windows Defender programs, and the anti-phishing and anti-spam features of Internet Explorer and Windows Live Mail.

User Account Password

Windows 7 security begins with assigning a password to each user account on the computer. This prevents unauthorized users from accessing the system, and it enables you to lock your computer. See "Protect an Account with a Password" and "Lock Your Computer," later in this chapter.

User Account Control

User Account Control asks you to confirm certain actions that could conceivably harm your system. If you have an administrator account, you click **Yes** to continue; if you have a standard account, you must enter an administrator's user name and password to continue.

Parental Controls

If one or more children use your computer, you can use Windows 7's Parental Controls to protect those children from inadvertently running certain programs, playing unsuitable games, and using the computer at inappropriate times. See "Set Up Parental Controls," later in this chapter.

Greg	
Standard user	
Password protected	
Time Limits:	On
Game Ratings:	Up to TEEN
Program Limits:	On

Windows Firewall

Because when your computer is connected to the Internet, it is possible for another person on the Internet to access your computer and infect it with a virus or cause other damage, Windows 7 comes with its Windows Firewall feature turned on. This prevents intruders from accessing your computer while you are online.

Windows Defender

Spyware is a software program that installs on your computer without your knowledge or consent. This program surreptitiously gathers data from your computer, steals your passwords, displays advertisements, and hijacks your Web browser. To prevent spyware from installing on your computer, Windows 7 includes the Windows Defender program.

Phishing

Phishing refers to e-mail messages or Web sites that appear to come from legitimate businesses and organizations, but actually come from a scam artist. The purpose of the message or site is to fool you into divulging personal or private data, such as passwords and credit card numbers. Internet Explorer and Windows Live Mail come with anti-phishing features to help prevent this.

Junk E-mail

Junk e-mail — or *spam* — refers to unsolicited, commercial e-mail messages that advertise anything from baldness cures to cheap printer cartridges. Many spams advertise deals that are simply fraudulent, and others feature such unsavory practices as linking to adult-oriented sites, and sites that install spyware. Windows Live Mail comes with a junk e-mail filter; see "Set the Junk E-mail Protection Level," later in this chapter.

Check Action Center for Security Problems

In Windows 7, the new Action Center displays messages about the current state of your PC. In particular, Action Center warns you if your computer has any current security problems.

For example, the Action Center tells you if your PC does not have virus protection installed, or if the Windows Defender spyware database is out of date or turned off. Action Center also warns you if User Account Control is turned off or if the Windows Firewall is deactivated.

Check Action Center for Security Problems

① Click **Start**.

② Click **Control Panel**.

The Control Panel window appears.

③ Click **Review your computer's status**.

The Action Center window appears.

④ Review the messages in the Security section.

⑤ Click a message button to resolve the security issue, such as clicking **Update now** if Windows Defender is out of date.

⑥ Click **Security**.

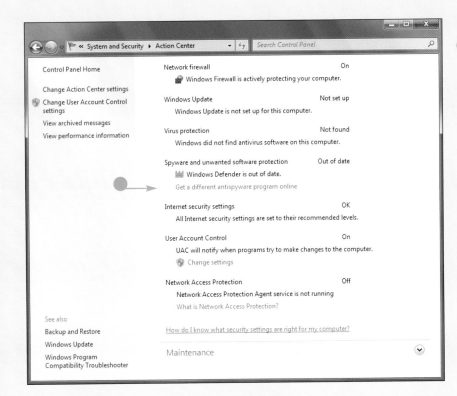

Control Panel Home

Change Action Center settings

Change User Account Control settings

View archived messages

View performance information

Network firewall — On
Windows Firewall is actively protecting your computer.

Windows Update — Not set up
Windows Update is not set up for this computer.

Virus protection — Not found
Windows did not find antivirus software on this computer.

Spyware and unwanted software protection — Out of date
Windows Defender is out of date.
Get a different antispyware program online

Internet security settings — OK
All Internet security settings are set to their recommended levels.

User Account Control — On
UAC will notify when programs try to make changes to the computer.
Change settings

Network Access Protection — Off
Network Access Protection Agent service is not running
What is Network Access Protection?

See also

Backup and Restore

Windows Update

Windows Program Compatibility Troubleshooter

How do I know what security settings are right for my computer?

Maintenance

⑦ Scroll down the Action Center window.

● Action Center displays a summary of all your system's security settings.

Simplify It

Is there a quicker way to see Action Center messages?
Yes, you can view Action Center messages and open the Action Center more quickly by following these steps:

① Click the **Action Center** icon (▣) in the taskbar's notification area.

● The current Action Center messages appear here.

② To launch Action Center, click **Open Action Center**.

2 important messages
3 total messages

Find an antivirus program online (Important)

Change Windows Update settings (Important)

Set up backup

Open Action Center ← ②

① ▣ 🔲 ◀) 10:20 AM 8/9/2009

Protect an Account with a Password

You can protect your Windows 7 user account with a password. This is a good idea because otherwise another user can log on to your account just by clicking your user name in the Welcome screen. Once you have a password associated with your user account, another user can still click your user name in the Welcome screen, but that person must then enter your password before Windows 7 goes any further.

For maximum security, make sure you create a strong password that cannot be easily guessed or hacked. See the tip on the next page.

Protect an Account with a Password

1 Click **Start**.

2 Click **Control Panel**.

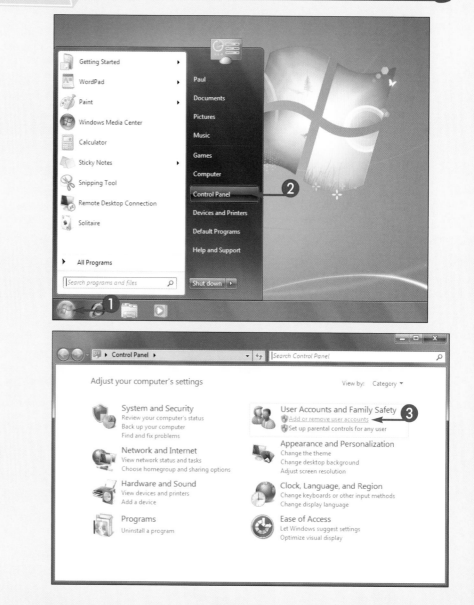

The Control Panel window appears.

3 Click **Add or remove user accounts**.

The Manage Accounts window appears.

④ Click the user account you want to work with.

The Change an Account window appears.

⑤ Click **Create a password**.

The Create Password window appears.

⑥ Type the password.

⑦ Type the password again.

⑧ Type a word or phrase to use as a password hint in case you forget the password.

⑨ Click **Create password**.

Windows 7 adds the password to the user account.

Simplify It

What are the components of a strong password?
First, do not use obvious items such as your name or a word such as "password." Your password should be at least eight characters long, and it should include at least one character from each of the following three sets: lowercase letters, uppercase letters, and numbers. The strongest passwords also include at least one symbol such as % or &.

How do I change the password?
Follow Steps **1** to **4** to open the Change an Account window. Click the **Change the password** link to open the Change Password dialog box. Type your existing password, follow Steps **6** to **8** to specify the new password and hint, and then click **Change password**.

Lock Your Computer

Protecting your account with a password prevents someone from logging on to your account, but what happens when you leave your desk? If you remain logged on to the system, any person who sits down at your computer can use it to view and change files.

To prevent this, lock your computer, which hides your desktop and displays the Windows 7 Welcome screen.

Once your computer is locked, anyone who tries to use your computer will first have to enter your password in the Welcome screen.

Lock Your Computer

LOCK YOUR COMPUTER

① Click **Start**.

② Click the power button arrow (▶).

③ Click **Lock**.

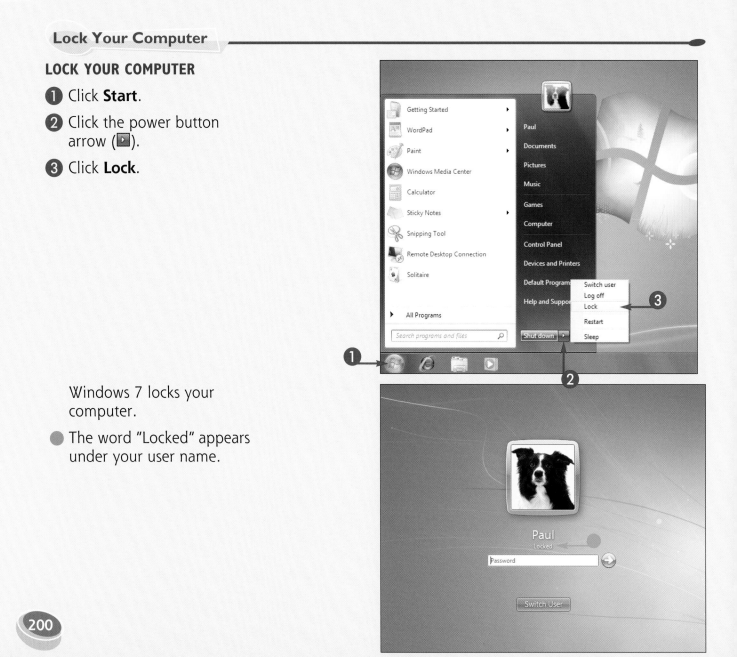

Windows 7 locks your computer.

● The word "Locked" appears under your user name.

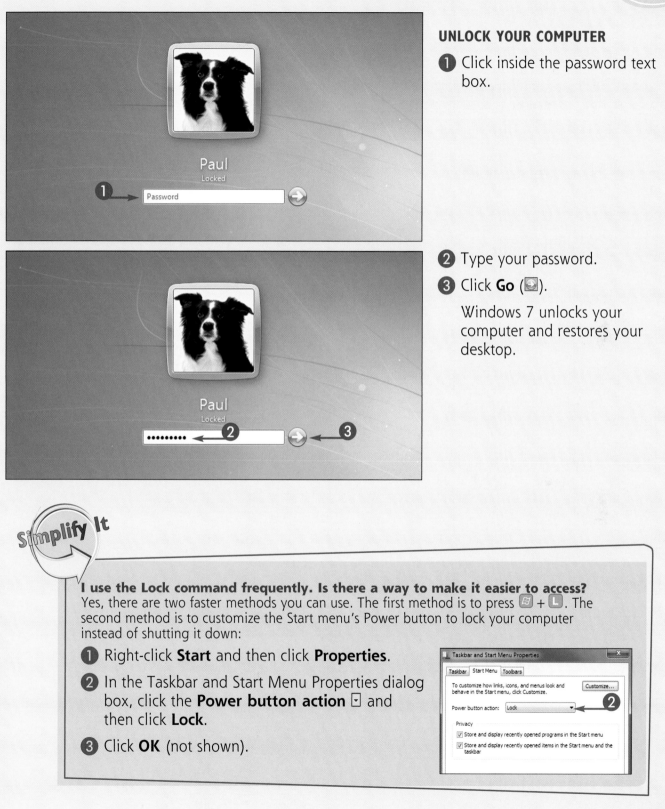

UNLOCK YOUR COMPUTER

1 Click inside the password text box.

2 Type your password.

3 Click **Go** (⬤).

Windows 7 unlocks your computer and restores your desktop.

Simplify It

I use the Lock command frequently. Is there a way to make it easier to access?
Yes, there are two faster methods you can use. The first method is to press ⊞ + L. The second method is to customize the Start menu's Power button to lock your computer instead of shutting it down:

1 Right-click **Start** and then click **Properties**.

2 In the Taskbar and Start Menu Properties dialog box, click the **Power button action** ⊡ and then click **Lock**.

3 Click **OK** (not shown).

Set Up Parental Controls

If your children have computer access, you can protect them from malicious content by setting up parental controls for their computer activities. With parental controls turned on, you can configure times when each child is allowed to use the computer. You can also set up controls on activities such as playing games and running programs.

Before you can apply parental controls, you must set up a Windows 7 user account for each child. See "Create a User Account" in Chapter 7.

Set Up Parental Controls

ACTIVATE PARENTAL CONTROLS

① Click **Start**.

② Click **Control Panel**.

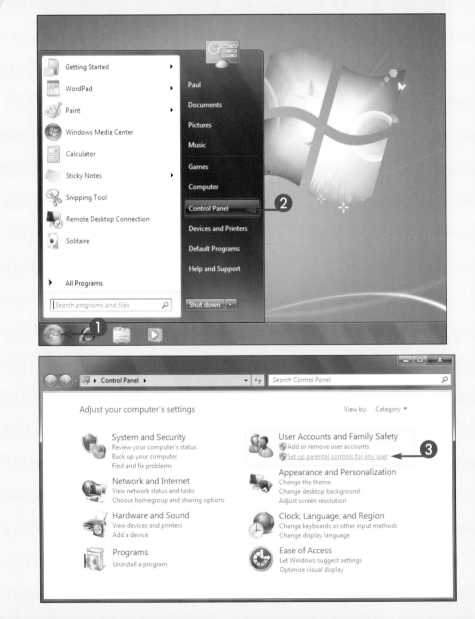

The Control Panel window appears.

③ Click **Set up parental controls for any user**.

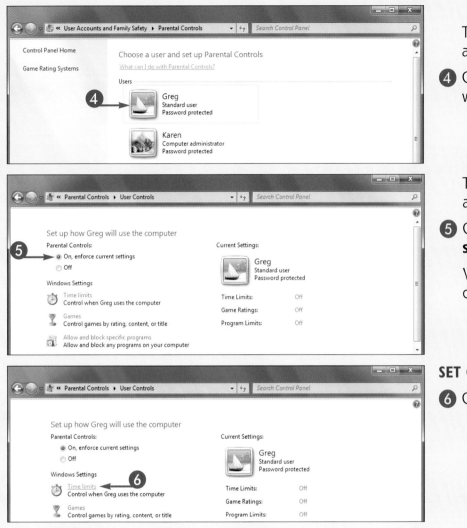

The Parental Controls window appears.

④ Click the user you want to work with.

The User Controls window appears.

⑤ Click **On, enforce current settings** (⊙ changes to ⦿).

Windows 7 turns on parental controls for the user.

SET COMPUTER TIME LIMITS

⑥ Click **Time limits**.

continued ▶

Simplify It

Can I use Parental Controls to monitor my kids' computer activities or restrict what they see on the Web?
No, activity reporting and Web filtering are not part of the default Parental Controls in Windows 7. However, these controls are available from third-party companies, and Microsoft provides links to them at http://windowshelp.microsoft.com. After you install a new control, it appears in the Parental Controls window in the Additional Controls section.

Can I choose which game rating system Windows 7 uses?
Yes, Windows 7 supports several game rating systems, including classifications from the Entertainment Software Rating Board (this is the default system), Computer Entertainment Rating Organization, and Game Rating Board. Return to the Parental Controls window, click **Game Rating Systems**, click the system you want to use (⊙ changes to ⦿), and then click **OK**.

Set Up Parental Controls *(continued)*

With parental controls activated, you can now set up specific restrictions. For example, you can set up times when children are allowed to use the computer and when computer use is forbidden.

Windows 7's parental controls also enable you to set the maximum game rating that kids can play, and you can block specific games. Parental controls also enable you to set up a list of programs that your children are allowed to use.

Set Up Parental Controls *(continued)*

The Time Restrictions window appears.

⑦ Click each hour that you want to block access to the computer.

● Blocked hours appear in blue.

● Allowed hours appear in white.

Note: *To block out a number of hours over a number of days, click and drag the mouse ⌖ over the hours.*

⑧ Click **OK**.

RESTRICT GAME USAGE

⑨ Click **Games**.

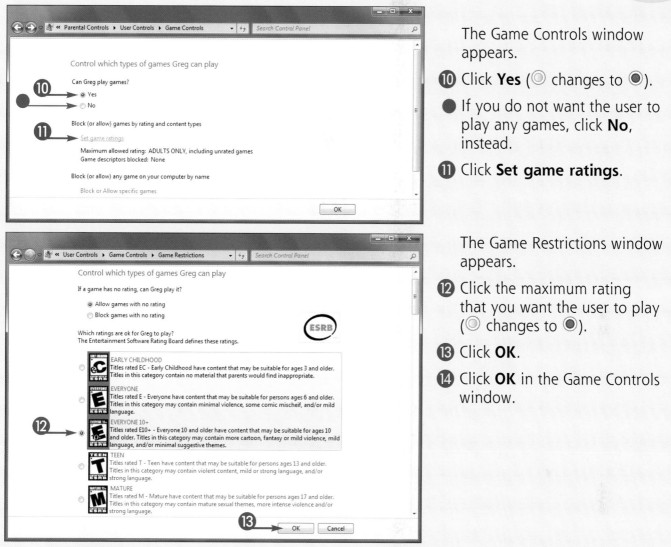

The Game Controls window appears.

⑩ Click **Yes** (⊙ changes to ⊙).

● If you do not want the user to play any games, click **No**, instead.

⑪ Click **Set game ratings**.

The Game Restrictions window appears.

⑫ Click the maximum rating that you want the user to play (⊙ changes to ⊙).

⑬ Click **OK**.

⑭ Click **OK** in the Game Controls window.

Simplify It

Can I block a specific game?
Yes. In the Game Controls window, click **Block or Allow specific games** to display the Game Overrides window, which shows all the games installed on your computer. For the game you want to block, click the **Always Block** option (⊙ changes to ⊙), and then click **OK**.

Can I prevent my kids from running certain programs?
Yes. In the User Controls window, click **Allow and block specific programs** to display the Application Restrictions dialog box. Click *User* **can only use the programs I allow** (where *User* is the name of the user). In the list, click the check box for each program you want the user to be able to run (☐ changes to ☑). Click **OK**.

Delete Your Browsing History

To ensure that other people who have access to your computer cannot view information from sites you have visited, you can delete your browsing history.

Internet Explorer maintains a list of the sites you visit, as well as copies of site content so that pages load faster the next time you view them. Internet Explorer also saves text and passwords that you have typed into forms, and *cookies*, which are small text files that store information

such as site preferences and logon data.

Saving this history makes surfing easier, but it is dangerous because other people who use your computer can just as easily visit or view information about those sites. This can be a problem if you visit financial sites, private corporate sites, or some other page that you would not want another person to visit. You reduce this risk by deleting some or all of your browsing history.

Delete Your Browsing History

① Click **Safety**.

② Click **Delete Browsing History**.

Note: *You can also press* Ctrl + Shift + Delete.

The Delete Browsing History dialog box appears.

③ To keep the browsing history associated with sites on your Favorites list, click **Preserve Favorites website data** (☐ changes to ☑).

④ To delete saved Web page files, click **Temporary Internet files** (☐ changes to ☑).

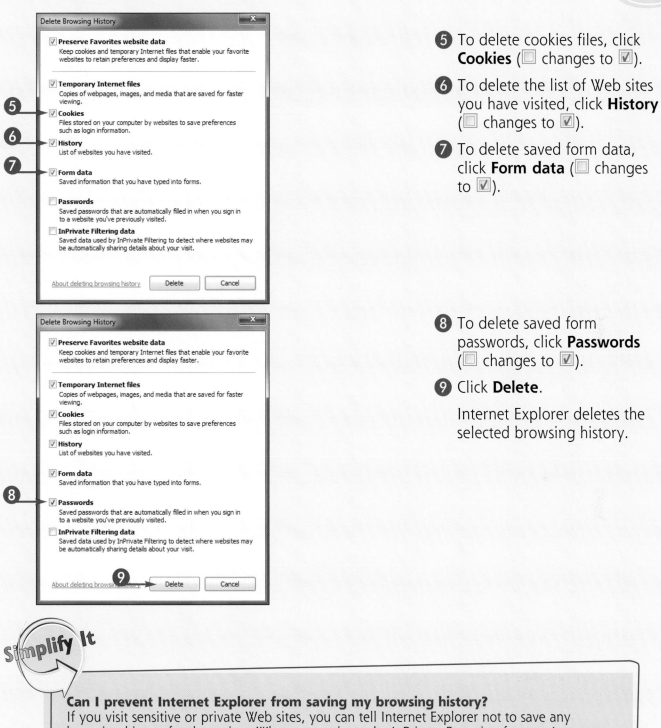

⑤ To delete cookies files, click **Cookies** (☐ changes to ☑).

⑥ To delete the list of Web sites you have visited, click **History** (☐ changes to ☑).

⑦ To delete saved form data, click **Form data** (☐ changes to ☑).

⑧ To delete saved form passwords, click **Passwords** (☐ changes to ☑).

⑨ Click **Delete**.

Internet Explorer deletes the selected browsing history.

Can I prevent Internet Explorer from saving my browsing history?
If you visit sensitive or private Web sites, you can tell Internet Explorer not to save any browsing history for those sites. When you activate the InPrivate Browsing feature, Internet Explorer stops saving browsing history when you visit Web sites. Internet Explorer also turns off third-party toolbars and other add-ons that you have added to the browser.

To turn on InPrivate Browsing, click **Safety** and then click **InPrivate Browsing**. (You can also press `Ctrl` + `Shift` + `P`.) A new Internet Explorer window appears, and you see [InPrivate] in the title bar, and the InPrivate indicator in the address bar.

Set the Junk E-mail Protection Level

You can make junk messages easier to manage by setting the Windows Live Mail junk e-mail protection level. You can set a higher level if you receive many junk messages each day, or you can set a lower level if you receive very few junk messages.

The higher the protection level, the more aggressively Windows Live Mail checks for junk e-mail. All suspected junk messages get moved to the Junk E-mail folder. If a legitimate message is moved to Junk E-mail by accident, you can mark the message as not junk.

Set the Junk E-mail Protection Level

SET THE JUNK E-MAIL PROTECTION LEVEL

① Click **Menus** (📑).

② Click **Safety options**.

The Safety Options dialog box appears.

③ Click the **Options** tab.

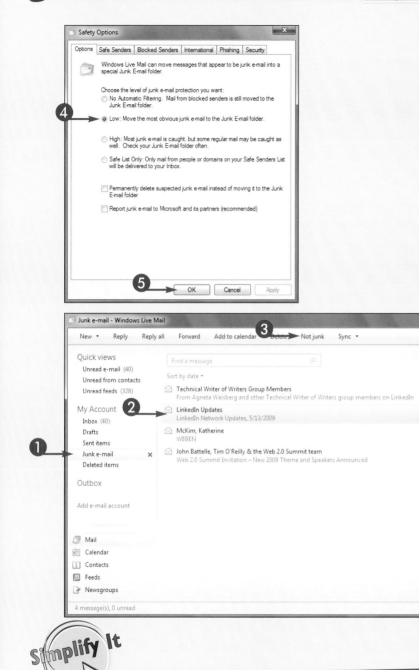

④ Click the protection level you want (◯ changes to ◉):

Click **No Automatic Filtering** if you receive very few junk messages each day.

Click **Low** if you receive a moderate number of junk messages.

Click **High** if you receive many junk messages each day.

⑤ Click **OK**.

Windows Live Mail puts the new protection level into effect.

MARK A MESSAGE AS NOT JUNK

① Click the Junk E-mail folder.

② Click the message.

③ Click **Not junk**.

Windows Mail returns the message to the Inbox folder.

Simplify It

What is a false positive?
A false positive is a legitimate message that Windows Live Mail has mistakenly marked as spam and moved to the Junk E-mail folder. If you select the High protection level, you run a greater risk of false positives, so you should check your Junk E-mail folder more often to look for legitimate messages.

How does the Safe List Only protection level work?
Safe List Only means that Windows Live Mail treats every message as junk, unless the sender's e-mail address is on your Safe Senders list. To populate this list, follow Steps **1** and **2**, click the **Safe Senders** tab, click **Add**, type an address, click **OK**, and repeat as necessary. Alternatively, right-click a legitimate message, click **Junk e-mail**, and then click **Add sender to safe senders list**.

Chapter 11

Customizing Windows 7

Windows 7 comes with a number of features that enable you to personalize your computer. For example, you can change the appearance of Windows 7 to suit your taste, including selecting a new desktop background, setting up a desktop slide show, choosing a screen saver, and changing the Windows 7 color scheme.

You can also change the way Windows 7 works to make it easier to use and more efficient. For example, you can change the icons that appear on the Start menu and you can configure the taskbar to make it easier to use.

Open the Personalization Window

To make changes to many of Windows 7's display options, you need to know how to open the Personalization window.

The Personalization window is one of the most powerful and useful features of Windows 7. With the Personalization window you can

change the desktop background, select a new color scheme, set up a screen saver, and more. With the Personalization window you can also apply themes to quickly and easily change the overall look of Windows 7.

Open the Personalization Window

1 Click **Start**.

2 Click **Control Panel**.

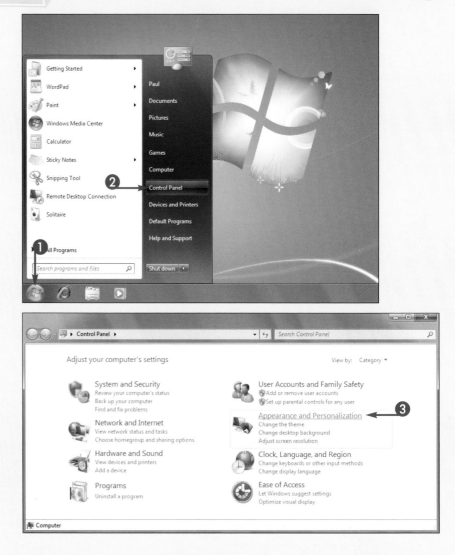

The Control Panel window appears.

3 Click **Appearance and Personalization**.

The Appearance and Personalization window appears.

④ Click **Personalization**.

The Personalization window appears.

Note: *A quicker way to open the Personalization window is to right-click an empty section of the desktop and then click* **Personalize***.*

⑤ Click the **Close** button (⊠) when you are finished working with this window.

Si**mplify It**

What is a theme?
The next few sections show you how to tweak the desktop background, screen saver, and color scheme. Instead of performing those tasks individually, you can change all of these at once by applying a theme. Each theme also includes its own set of desktop icons, sound effects, and mouse pointers. In the Personalization window, scroll down to view the available themes, and then click the theme you want to use.

Can I create my own theme?
Yes. After you have customized the desktop background, screen saver, and color scheme, you can save all of these changes as a custom theme. In the Personalization window, click **Unsaved Theme** and then click **Save theme**. In the Save Theme As dialog box, use the Theme Name text box to type a name for your theme, and then click **Save**.

Change the Desktop Background

For a different look, you can change the desktop background to display either a different image or a specific color.

Windows 7 comes with more than three dozen desktop background images, which includes scenes of nature, architectural photos, fantasy characters, and more. If none of the built-in desktop backgrounds appeal to you, you can also use one of your own photos as the background.

You can also display multiple desktop images as a slide show. See "Set Up a Desktop Slide Show," later in this chapter.

Change the Desktop Background

① Open the Personalization window.

Note: See the "Open the Personalization Window" section earlier in this chapter.

② Click **Desktop Background**.

The Desktop Background window appears.

③ Click the **Picture location** ⊡ and then click the background gallery you want to use.

Note: If you have your own image that you would prefer to use as the desktop background, click **Pictures Library** in the list. You can also click Browse and then use the Browse dialog box to select the file.

● Windows 7 displays the backgrounds in the selected gallery.

④ Click **Clear all**.

⑤ Click the image or color you want to use.

⑥ Click the **Picture position** ⊡ and then click the positioning you want.

Note: See the tip, below, for an explanation of each option.

⑦ Click **Save changes**.

⑧ Click the **Close** button (⊠).

The picture or color you selected appears on the desktop.

Simplify It

What is the difference between the five Picture position options?

● **Fill**: Displays a single copy of the image extended on all sides so it fills the entire desktop. As it extends the picture, Windows keeps the ratio of width to height the same, so this usually means that part of the image gets cut off.

● **Fit**: Displays a single copy of the image extended until either the width of the picture fits the width of the screen, or the height of the picture fits the height of the screen. Use this position if you want to display all of the image without distortion and without cutting off any of the image.

● **Stretch**: Displays a single copy of the image extended on all sides so it fills the entire desktop. In this case, Windows does not keep the ratio of the width to height, so your picture may end up a bit distorted.

● **Tile**: Displays multiple copies of the image repeated so they fill the entire desktop. Choose this option for small images.

● **Center**: Displays a single copy of the image in the center of the screen. This is a good choice for large images.

Set Up a Desktop Slide Show

You can add visual interest to your desktop by configuring Windows 7 to display a slide show of images as the desktop background. This means that Windows 7 changes the desktop background automatically at a preset time interval.

You set up the slide show by selecting multiple images that you want to appear on the desktop. You then set up the time interval you want Windows 7 to use to change from one image to the next. You can choose an interval as short as ten seconds or as long as one day.

Set Up a Desktop Slide Show

1 Open the Personalization window.

Note: See the "Open the Personalization Window" section earlier in this chapter.

2 Click **Desktop Background**.

The Desktop Background window appears.

3 Click the **Picture location** ☐ and then click the background gallery you want to use.

Note: If you have your own image that you would prefer to use as the desktop background, click **Pictures Library** in the list. You can also click **Browse** and then use the Browse dialog box to select the file.

● Windows 7 displays the backgrounds in the selected gallery and selects all the images.

If you want to use all the images in the gallery, skip to Step **6**.

④ Click **Clear all**.

⑤ For each image you want to include in the slide show, position the mouse ⌖ over the image and click the check box (☐ changes to ☑).

⑥ Click the **Change picture every** ⊡ and then click the time interval between pictures.

⑦ To display the pictures in random order, click **Shuffle** (☐ changes to ☑).

⑧ Click **Save changes**.

Windows 7 displays the first picture on the desktop and displays new images using the interval you selected.

Simplify It

Can I control the playback of the desktop slide show?
Yes, but Windows 7 gives you only very limited control over the playback. For example, if you do not like the currently displayed image, right-click the desktop and then click **Next desktop background**. Windows 7 immediately changes the background to the next image in the slide show. Unfortunately, you cannot pause the slide show or return to a previous image.

Are there more background images available online?
Yes, Microsoft has a large number of desktop background images available on its Web site. In the Personalization window, click the **Get more themes online** link, and then click the **Desktop backgrounds** tab in the Web page that appears. For each background you want to use, click the **Download** link to open the picture in Internet Explorer, click **Page**, and then click **Save As**.

Set the Screen Saver

You can set up Windows 7 to display a *screen saver*, a moving pattern or series of pictures. The screen saver appears after your computer has been idle for a while.

If you leave your monitor on for long stretches while your computer is idle, the unmoving image can end up temporarily "burned" into the monitor's screen. A screen saver prevents this by displaying a moving image.

However, the temporarily burned image will not damage your monitor over the long term, so many people set up a screen saver to have something interesting to look at while their computer is idle.

Set the Screen Saver

① Open the Personalization window.

Note: *See the "Open the Personalization Window" section earlier in this chapter.*

② Click **Screen Saver**.

The Screen Saver Settings dialog box appears.

③ Click the **Screen saver** ⊡ and then click the screen saver you want to use.

● A preview of the screen saver appears.

Note: *Not all screen savers can display the small preview. To see an actual preview, click **Preview**. When you are done, move the mouse ⬚ or press a key to stop the preview.*

④ Click the **Wait** ⬍ to specify the number of minutes of computer idle time after which the screen saver appears.

⑤ Click **OK**.

The screen saver appears after your computer is idle for the number of minutes you specified in Step **4**.

Note: To interrupt the screen saver, move the mouse ⬉ or press Shift *on the keyboard.*

Simplify It

Can I use a screen saver to hide my work while I am away from my desk?
Yes. By itself, the screen saver's pattern automatically obscures the screen. However, another person can interrupt the screen saver to see your work. To prevent this, first assign a password to your Windows 7 user account, as described in the "Protect an Account with a Password" section in Chapter 10. In the Screen Saver tab, click the **On resume, display logon screen** check box (☐ changes to ☑). This means that anyone who interrupts the screen saver can see your work only if he or she knows your password.

Change the Windows 7 Color Scheme

You can personalize your copy of Windows 7 by choosing a different color scheme, which Windows 7 applies to the window borders, taskbar, and Start menu.

You can also customize the Windows 7 look by toggling the transparent glass effect on and off and by setting the color intensity. Windows 7 also enables you to create your own colors, each of which is a combination of three properties: hue (the color), saturation (the purity of the color), and brightness (how much gray is mixed in with the color).

Change the Windows 7 Color Scheme

① Open the Personalization window.

Note: See the "Open the Personalization Window" section earlier in this chapter.

② Click **Window Color**.

The Window Color and Appearance window appears.

Note: If you see the Window Color and Appearance dialog box, instead, see the tip on the next page.

③ Click the color you want to use.

● Windows 7 changes the color of the window border.

④ If you do not want to see the glass effect, click **Enable transparency** (☑ changes to ☐).

⑤ Click and drag the **Color intensity** slider to set the color intensity.

● Windows 7 changes the transparency and intensity of the window border.

⑥ Click **Show color mixer**.

● The color mixer sliders appear.

⑦ Click and drag the **Hue**, **Saturation**, and **Brightness** sliders to set your custom color.

⑧ Click **Save changes**.

Windows 7 applies the new color scheme.

Simplify It

Why do I see the Window Color and Appearance dialog box instead of the Window Color and Appearance window?
On systems with lower-end graphics cards or little graphics memory, Windows 7 is unable to use high-end effects such as transparency and color intensity. On such systems, you follow these steps to set the color scheme:

① In the Item list, click the interface object you want to customize.

② Click ⊡ in each Color list and select a color or colors for the item.

③ If the item includes text, use the Font, Size, Color, Bold, and Italics controls to format the text.

④ Repeat Steps **1** to **3** to customize other items.

⑤ Click **OK**.

221

Customize the Start Menu

You can personalize how the Start menu looks and operates to suit your style and the way you work. For example, you can turn off the lists of recently used documents and programs for privacy.

You can also control the items that appear on the right side of the menu. For example, you

can add and remove items, and you can change whether some items appear as links or menus.

You can also customize the number of recent programs that appear on the Start menu and the number of items that appear in jump lists.

Customize the Start Menu

① Right-click **Start**.

② Click **Properties**.

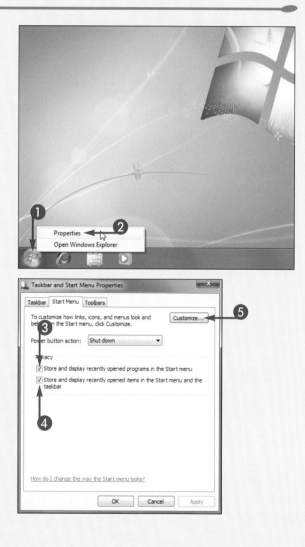

The Taskbar and Start Menu Properties dialog box appears with the Start Menu tab displayed.

③ If you do not want Windows 7 to list your recently used programs, click here (☑ changes to ☐).

④ If you do not want Windows 7 to list your recently used documents, click here (☑ changes to ☐).

⑤ Click **Customize**.

The Customize Start Menu dialog box appears.

⑥ Use the Start menu items list to control the icons that appear on the right side of the Start menu.

● Some items have several option buttons that control how they appear on the Start menu; click the option you want (◎ changes to ◉).

● Some items have check boxes that determine whether the item appears (☑) or does not appear (☐) on the Start menu.

⑦ Click 🔼 to change the maximum number of your recent programs that can appear on the Start menu. (Select a number between 0 and 30.)

⑧ Click 🔼 to change the maximum number of the recent items that can appear in jump lists. (Select a number between 0 and 60.)

⑨ Click **OK**.

⑩ Click **OK**.

Windows 7 puts your new Start menu settings into effect.

Simplify It

Can I remove a program that appears on my Start menu's list of most often used programs?
Yes. Click **Start** to open the Start menu, and then right-click the program that you want to remove. In the shortcut menu that appears, click **Remove from this list**. Windows 7 removes the program's icon from the Start menu.

Can I add a program permanently to the Start menu?
Yes, you can *pin* a program so that it always appears at or near the top of the Start menu. Click **Start** to open the Start menu, and then right-click the program that you want to pin. In the shortcut menu, click **Pin to Start Menu**. The program's icon now appears in the top part of the menu, above the list of frequently used programs.

Customize the Taskbar

You can personalize how the taskbar operates and looks to make it more efficient and suit your working style.

For example, you can unlock the taskbar, which enables you to change the size of the taskbar, such as making the taskbar taller to make the

icons appear less crowded. You can also temporarily hide the taskbar to give your programs more room on the desktop. You can also display smaller taskbar icons, which enables you to fit more icons on the taskbar.

Customize the Taskbar

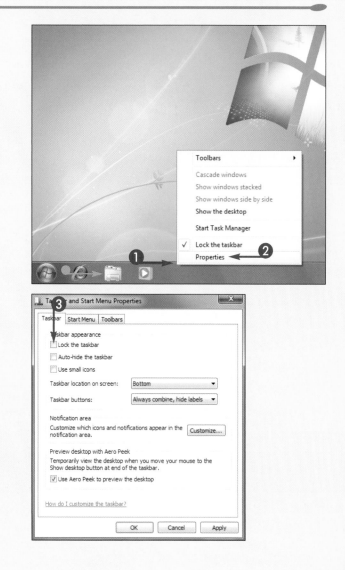

- You can click and drag a taskbar icon to move it to a different location.

1 Right-click an empty section of the taskbar.

2 Click **Properties**.

The Taskbar and Start Menu Properties dialog box appears with the Taskbar tab displayed.

3 Click **Lock the taskbar** (☑ changes to ☐) to unlock the taskbar.

Note: Unlocking the taskbar enables you resize the taskbar.

*Note: To quickly lock and unlock the taskbar, right-click an empty section of the taskbar and click **Lock the taskbar**.*

Taskbar and Start Menu Properties

Taskbar | Start Menu | Toolbars

Taskbar appearance

☐ Lock the taskbar

☑ Auto-hide the taskbar

☐ Use small icons

Taskbar location on screen: Bottom

Taskbar buttons: Always combine, hide labels

Notification area

Customize which icons and notifications appear in the notification area. [Customize...]

Preview desktop with Aero Peek

Temporarily view the desktop when you move your mouse to the Show desktop button at end of the taskbar.

☑ Use Aero Peek to preview the desktop

How do I customize the taskbar?

[OK] [Cancel] [Apply]

Taskbar and Start Menu Properties

Taskbar | Start Menu | Toolbars

Taskbar appearance

☐ Lock the taskbar

☑ Auto-hide the taskbar

☑ Use small icons

Taskbar location on screen: Bottom

Taskbar buttons: Always combine, hide labels

Notification area

Customize which icons and notifications appear in the notification area. [Customize...]

Preview desktop with Aero Peek

Temporarily view the desktop when you move your mouse to the Show desktop button at end of the taskbar.

☑ Use Aero Peek to preview the desktop

How do I customize the taskbar?

[OK] [Cancel] [Apply]

④ Click **Auto-hide the taskbar** (☐ changes to ☑) to hide the taskbar when you are using a program.

Note: *Auto-hiding the taskbar gives you more room on the desktop to display your program windows.*

Note: *To display the hidden taskbar, move the mouse ⊳ to the bottom edge of the screen.*

⑤ Click **Use small icons** (☐ changes to ☑) to use smaller versions of the taskbar icons.

Note: *Switching to smaller icons enables you to fit more icons on the taskbar.*

Simplify It

How do I resize the taskbar?
To resize the taskbar, first make sure you have followed Steps **1** to **3** (and then clicked **OK**) to unlock the taskbar. Click and drag the top edge of the taskbar up to get more taskbar rows. If you later find that the taskbar is too big, click and drag the top edge of the taskbar down to get fewer taskbar rows.

What is Aero Peek?
Aero Peek is a new Windows 7 feature that enables you to temporarily hide all your open windows to see the desktop. This is useful if you have gadgets on the desktop that you want to quickly view. When you activate the **Use Aero Peek to preview the desktop** check box (☐ changes to ☑), position your mouse pointer over the right edge of the taskbar to view the desktop.

Customize the Taskbar *(continued)*

To further personalize your taskbar, the Taskbar tab of the Taskbar and Start Menu Properties dialog box offers several other customization options. For example, you can change the taskbar location to the top of the screen or to the left or right side of the screen. You can also group taskbar buttons from the same application, which gives you more room to display other taskbar icons. Finally, you can also customize the notification area icons to determine which ones are hidden and which of the system icons you want to display.

Customize the Taskbar *(continued)*

6 Click the **Taskbar location on screen** ⊡ and then click the location you prefer: Bottom, Left, Right, or Top.

7 Click the **Taskbar buttons** ⊡ and then click the grouping option you prefer.

Note: *See the tip on the next page to learn about the various grouping options.*

8 Click **Customize**.

The Notification Area Icons window appears.

⑨ For each notification area icon, click ⊡ and then click the setting you prefer.

Note: See the tip below to learn about the various settings.

● If you choose to hide one or more notification area icons, you can click here to display the hidden icons.

● You can click this link to turn the system icons on or off.

⑩ Click **OK**.

⑪ Click **OK**.

Simplify It

What do the different taskbar grouping options mean?
Grouping taskbar buttons means showing only a single button for a program that has multiple windows open. To switch to one of those windows, click the taskbar button and then click the window name. **Always combine, hide labels** means that Windows 7 always groups buttons; **Combine when taskbar is full** means that Windows 7 waits until the taskbar is full before grouping; and **Never combine** disables grouping.

What do the different options for the notification area icons mean?
These options control whether the icon appears in the notification area and whether you see messages from the icon's program. Choose **Show icon and notifications** to see both the icon and its messages; choose **Only show notifications** to hide the icon but still see the messages; or choose **Hide icons and notifications** to hide the icon and not show the messages.

Chapter 12

Maintaining Windows 7

To keep your system running smoothly, maintain top performance, and reduce the risk of computer problems, you need to perform some routine maintenance chores. This chapter shows you the most important of those chores, with an emphasis on maintaining your hard drive. For example, you learn how to monitor your hard drive's available space, delete unnecessary files to free up hard drive space, defragment your hard drive for better performance, and how to check your hard drive for errors.

In this chapter you also learn how to back up your files and how to restore files from your backups.

Check Hard Drive Free Space

You can check how much free space your hard drive has. This is important because if you run out of room on your hard drive, you cannot install more programs or create more documents.

Of particular concern is the hard drive on which Windows 7 is installed, usually drive C. If this hard drive's free space gets low — say, less than 20 percent of the total hard drive space — Windows 7 runs slowly and may also experience problems, such as freezing.

Check Hard Drive Free Space

1 Click **Start**.

2 Click **Computer**.

Note: *You can also check the free space on CDs, DVDs, memory cards, or flash drives. Before you continue, insert the disc, card, or drive.*

The Computer window appears.

3 Click the **View** icon ▢.

4 Click **Tiles**.

● Information about each drive appears along with the drive icon.

● This value tells you the amount of free space on the drive.

● This value tells you the total amount of space on the drive.

● This bar gives you a visual indication of how much disk space is used on the drive.

● The used portion of the bar appears blue when a drive still has sufficient disk space.

● The used portion of the bar turns red when a drive's disk space becomes low.

⑤ Click the **Close** button (☒) to close the Computer window.

Simplify It

How often should I check my hard drive free space?
With normal computer use, you should check your hard drive free space about once a month. If you install programs, create large files, or download media frequently, you should probably check your free space every couple of weeks.

What can I do if my hard drive space is getting low?
You can do three things:

● **Delete Documents**. If you have documents — particularly media files such as images, music, and videos — that you are sure you no longer need, delete them.

● **Remove Programs**. If you have programs that you no longer use, uninstall them (see "Uninstall a Program" in Chapter 2).

● **Run Disk Cleanup**. Use the Disk Cleanup program to delete files that Windows 7 no longer uses. See the next section, "Delete Unnecessary Files."

Delete Unnecessary Files

To free up hard drive space on your computer and keep Windows 7 running efficiently, you can use the Disk Cleanup program to delete files that your system no longer needs.

With Disk Cleanup you can remove downloaded program files, temporary Internet files, Recycle Bin files, temporary Windows files, and more.

Run Disk Cleanup any time that your hard drive free space gets too low. If hard drive space is not a problem, run Disk Cleanup every two or three months.

Delete Unnecessary Files

① Click **Start**.

② Click **All Programs**.

   *Note: When you click **All Programs**, the command name changes to Back.*

③ Click **Accessories**.

④ Click **System Tools**.

⑤ Click **Disk Cleanup**.

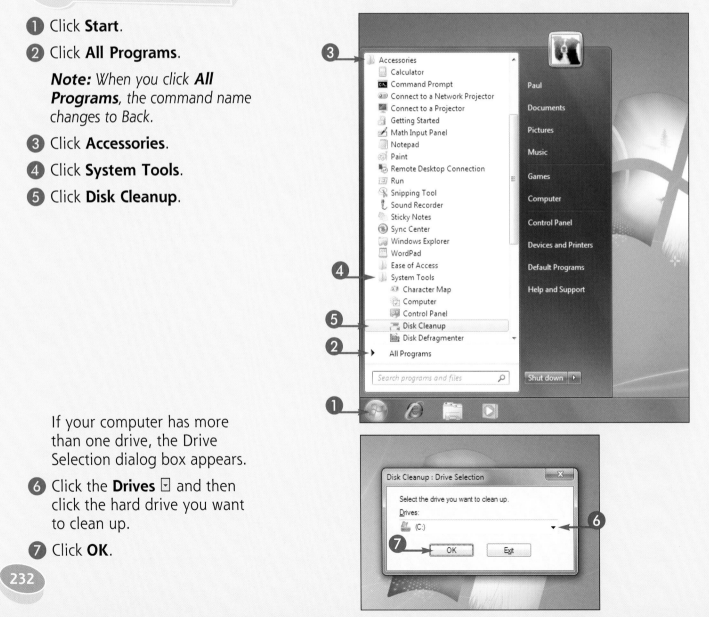

If your computer has more than one drive, the Drive Selection dialog box appears.

⑥ Click the **Drives** ⊡ and then click the hard drive you want to clean up.

⑦ Click **OK**.

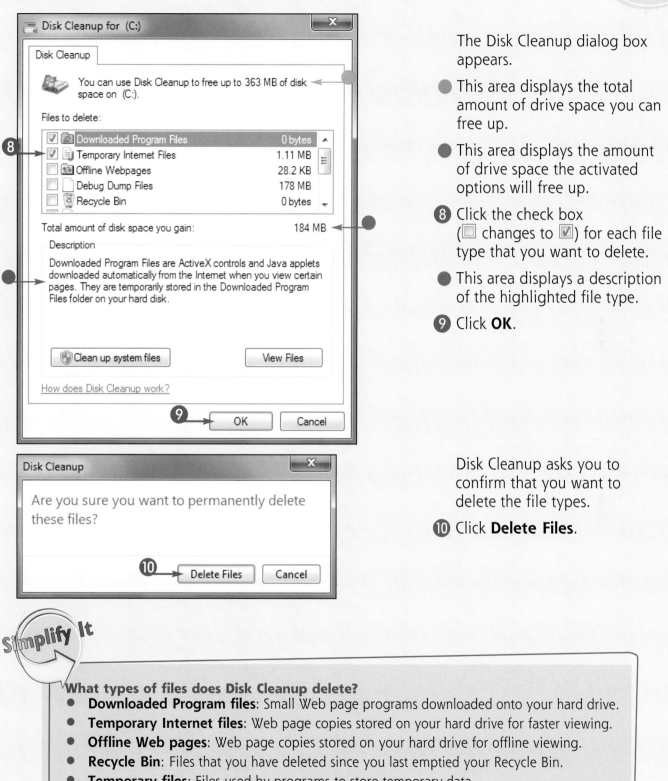

The Disk Cleanup dialog box appears.

● This area displays the total amount of drive space you can free up.

● This area displays the amount of drive space the activated options will free up.

⑧ Click the check box (☐ changes to ☑) for each file type that you want to delete.

● This area displays a description of the highlighted file type.

⑨ Click **OK**.

Disk Cleanup asks you to confirm that you want to delete the file types.

⑩ Click **Delete Files**.

Simplify It

What types of files does Disk Cleanup delete?
- **Downloaded Program files**: Small Web page programs downloaded onto your hard drive.
- **Temporary Internet files**: Web page copies stored on your hard drive for faster viewing.
- **Offline Web pages**: Web page copies stored on your hard drive for offline viewing.
- **Recycle Bin**: Files that you have deleted since you last emptied your Recycle Bin.
- **Temporary files**: Files used by programs to store temporary data.
- **Thumbnails**: Miniature versions of images and other content used in folder windows.

233

Defragment Your Hard Drive on a Schedule

You can make Windows 7, and your programs, run faster, and your documents open more quickly, by defragmenting your hard drive on a regular schedule.

Most files are stored on your computer in several pieces, and over time, those pieces often get scattered around your hard drive,

which means your hard drive becomes fragmented. This slows down your computer because Windows 7 has to spend extra time locating and opening each piece of a file. Defragmenting improves performance by bringing all those pieces together, making finding and opening each file faster.

Defragment Your Hard Drive on a Schedule

1 Click **Start**.

2 Click **All Programs**.

Note: When you click **All Programs**, the command name changes to Back.

3 Click **Accessories**.

4 Click **System Tools**.

5 Click **Disk Defragmenter**.

The Disk Defragmenter window appears.

6 Click **Configure schedule**.

Disk Defragmenter: Modify Schedule

Disk defragmenter schedule configuration:

⑦ ☑ Run on a schedule (recommended)

Frequency: Monthly ⑧

Day: 1 ⑨

Time: 3:00 AM ⑩

Disks: Select disks...

⑪ OK   Cancel

Disk Defragmenter

Disk Defragmenter consolidates fragmented files on your computer's hard disk to improve system performance. Tell me more about Disk Defragmenter.

Schedule:

Scheduled defragmentation is turned on
Run at 3:00 AM on day 1 of every month
Next scheduled run: 6/1/2009 3:00 AM

Configure schedule...

Current status:

Disk	Last Run	Progress
(C:)	5/20/2009 2:56 AM (0% fragmented)	
Data (D:)	5/20/2009 2:57 AM (0% fragmented)	
(L:)	5/20/2009 2:56 AM (0% fragmented)	
System Reserved	5/20/2009 2:56 AM (0% fragmented)	

Only disks that can be defragmented are shown.
To best determine if your disks need defragmenting right now, you need to first analyze your disks.

Analyze disk   Defragment disk

⑫ Close

The Disk Defragmenter: Modify Schedule dialog box appears.

⑦ Click **Run on a schedule (recommended)** (☐ changes to ☑).

⑧ Click the **Frequency** ⊡ and then click the frequency with which you want to defragment (Daily, Weekly, or Monthly).

⑨ Click the **Day** ⊡ and click either the day of the week (for a Weekly schedule) or the day of the month (for a Monthly schedule).

⑩ Click the **Time** ⊡ and then click the time of day to run the defragment.

⑪ Click **OK**.

● The new schedule appears here.

● If you want to defragment your drives now, click **Defragment disk**.

⑫ Click **Close**.

Simplify It

How often should I defragment my hard drive?
This depends on how often you use your computer. If you use your computer every day, you should defragment your hard drive weekly. If you use your computer only occasionally, you should defragment your hard drive monthly.

How long will defragmenting my hard drive take?
It depends on the size of the hard drive, the amount of data on it, and the extent of the defragmentation. Budget at least 15 minutes for the defragment, and know that it could take more than an hour.

235

Check Your Hard Drive for Errors

Because hard drive errors can cause files to become corrupted, which may prevent you from running a program or opening a document, you can use the Check Disk program to look for and fix hard drive errors.

A standard Check Disk operation makes sure that each of your files and folders is accessible and readable. However, you can also perform a more thorough check that examines the hard drive itself to look for physical errors in the drive.

Check Your Hard Drive for Errors

1 Click **Start**.

2 Click **Computer** (not shown).

The Computer window appears.

3 Click the hard drive that you want to check.

4 Click **Properties**.

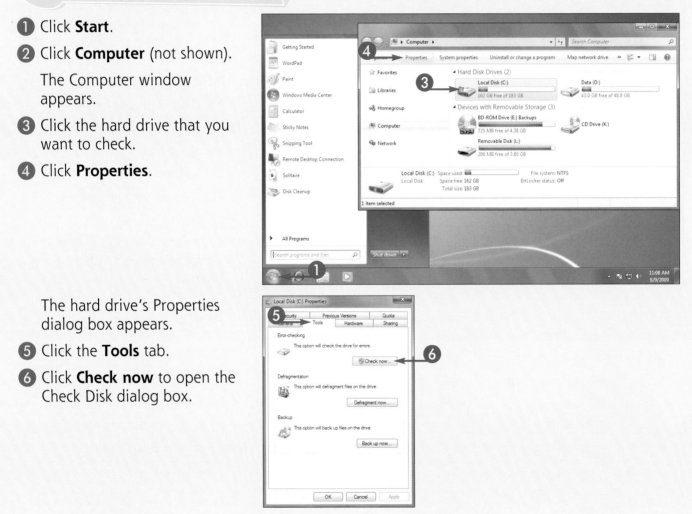

The hard drive's Properties dialog box appears.

5 Click the **Tools** tab.

6 Click **Check now** to open the Check Disk dialog box.

Check Disk Local Disk (C:)

Check disk options

☑ Automatically fix file system errors
☐ Scan for and attempt recovery of bad sectors

Start   Cancel

Microsoft Windows

Windows can't check the disk while it's in use

Do you want to check for hard disk errors the next time you start your computer?

Schedule disk check   Cancel

Local Disk (C:) Properties

Security	Previous Versions	Quota
General	Tools	Hardware	Sharing

Error-checking

This option will check the drive for errors.

Check now...

Defragmentation

This option will defragment files on the drive.

Defragment now...

Backup

This option will back up files on the drive.

Back up now...

OK   Cancel   Apply

⑦ If you want Check Disk to fix any errors it finds, click **Automatically fix file system errors** (☐ changes to ☑).

⑧ If you want Check Disk to look for bad sectors, check **Scan for and attempt recovery of bad sectors** (☐ changes to ☑).

⑨ Click **Start**.

If you are checking the drive where Windows 7 is installed, Check Disk asks whether you want to check the disk the next time you start your computer.

⑩ Click **Schedule disk check**.

⑪ Click **OK**.

Windows 7 checks your hard drive the next time you start your computer.

Note: If Check Disk finds any errors and you did not click the **Automatically fix file system errors** option in Step **7**, follow the instructions provided by the program.

Simplify It

What is a "bad sector"?
A *sector* is a small storage location on your hard drive. When Windows 7 saves a file on the drive, it divides the file into pieces and stores each piece in a separate sector. A bad sector is one that, through physical damage or some other cause, can no longer be used to reliably store data.

How often should I check for hard drive errors?
You should perform the basic hard drive check about once a week. Perform the more thorough bad sector check once a month. Note that the bad sector check can take several hours, depending on the size of the drive, so perform this check only when you will not need your computer for a while.

Back Up Files

You can use the Windows Backup program to make backup copies of your important files. If a system problem causes you to lose one or more files, you can restore them from the backup.

To set up Windows 7 for backups, you run through a short configuration procedure. Once that is done, you do not have to worry about backups again because Windows 7 handles everything for you automatically.

In the Windows Backup program, you can back up to a recordable CD or DVD drive, to another hard drive on your system, or to a network location.

Back Up Files

① Click **Start**.

② Click **All Programs**.

Note: When you click **All Programs**, the command name changes to Back.

③ Click **Maintenance**.

④ Click **Backup and Restore**.

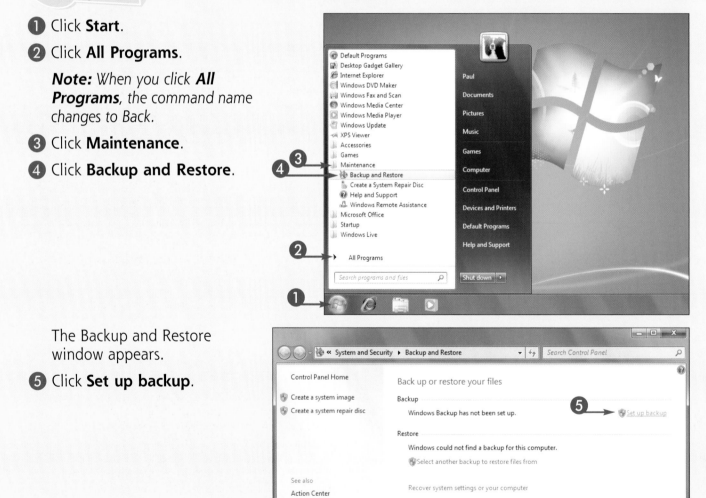

The Backup and Restore window appears.

⑤ Click **Set up backup**.

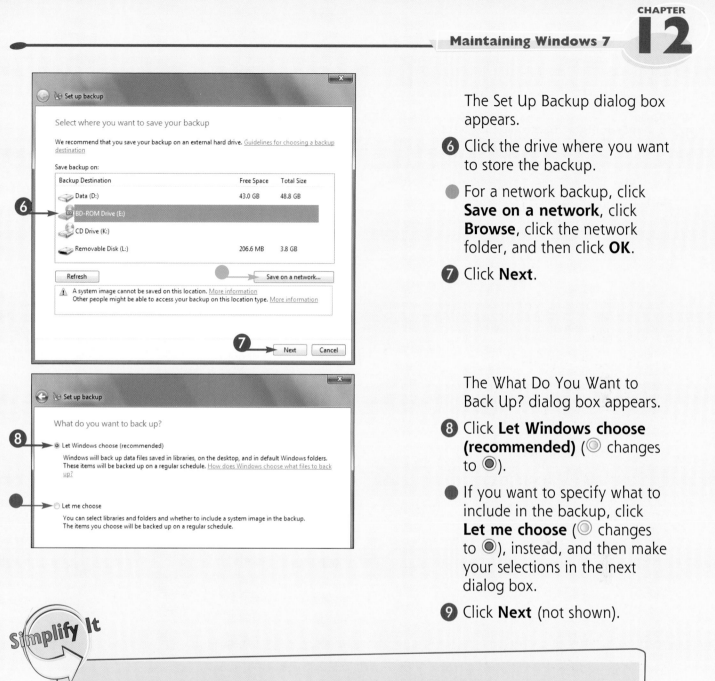

The Set Up Backup dialog box appears.

⑥ Click the drive where you want to store the backup.

● For a network backup, click **Save on a network**, click **Browse**, click the network folder, and then click **OK**.

⑦ Click **Next**.

The What Do You Want to Back Up? dialog box appears.

⑧ Click **Let Windows choose (recommended)** (◎ changes to ◉).

● If you want to specify what to include in the backup, click **Let me choose** (◎ changes to ◉), instead, and then make your selections in the next dialog box.

⑨ Click **Next** (not shown).

Simplify It

I just created some important documents. Can I back up right away?
Yes. First you must complete the steps in this section to perform at least one backup and set your backup configuration. Now, whenever you need to perform a backup, follow Steps **1** to **4** to display the Backup and Restore window, and then click **Back up now**.

What is a system image?
A system image is an exact copy of your entire system. This type of backup includes not only your documents, but also your programs, your Windows 7 configuration, and all the Windows 7 files. If your computer crashes and will no longer start, you can use a system image backup to restore the entire system. If you back up to another hard drive or a network drive, a system image is automatically included in the backup.

continued

Back Up
Files *(continued)*

By default, Windows Backup backs up the files in your Windows 7 libraries: Documents, Music, Pictures, and Video, as well as your favorites, contacts, e-mail, downloads, saved searches, and the contents of your desktop. Windows Backup also backs up the library files for the other users on your computer.

Note that you need to run through these configuration steps only once. After you have configured your initial backup, Windows Backup runs automatically once a week, although you can change that schedule if you prefer to back up more or less often.

Back Up Files *(continued)*

The Review Your Backup Settings dialog box appears.

⑩ Click **Save settings and run backup**.

Set up backup

Review your backup settings

Backup Location: BD-ROM Drive (E:)

Backup Summary:

Items	Included in backup
👥 All users	Default Windows folders and lo...

Schedule: Every Sunday at 7:00 PM Change schedule

⑩ → Save settings and run backup   Cancel

If you are backing up to a CD or DVD, Windows Backup asks you to insert a blank disk.

⑪ Insert a blank disc in the drive.

⑫ Click **OK**.

Back Up Files

Label and insert a blank media

Please write the following label on a blank media and insert it into E:\

MEDIAPC 5/25/2009 12:25 PM Drive 1

⑫ → OK   Stop backup

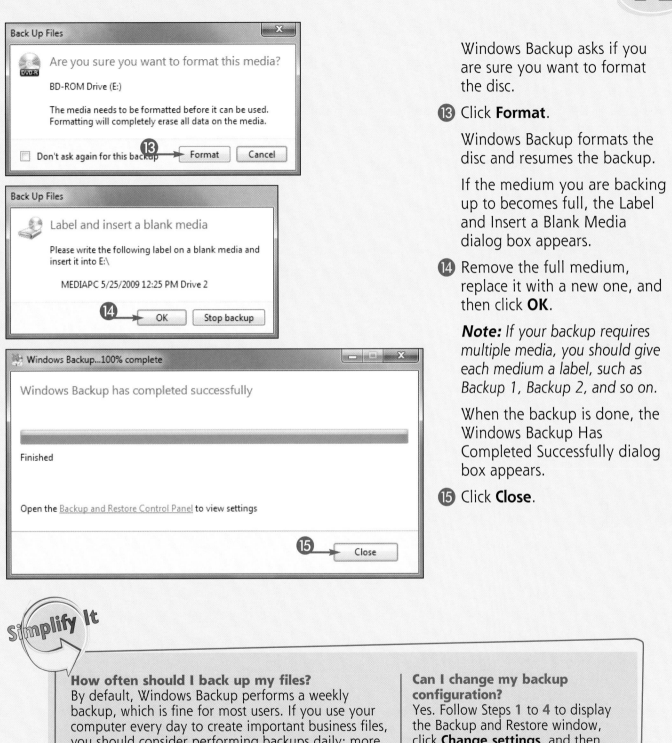

Windows Backup asks if you are sure you want to format the disc.

⑬ Click **Format**.

Windows Backup formats the disc and resumes the backup.

If the medium you are backing up to becomes full, the Label and Insert a Blank Media dialog box appears.

⑭ Remove the full medium, replace it with a new one, and then click **OK**.

Note: *If your backup requires multiple media, you should give each medium a label, such as Backup 1, Backup 2, and so on.*

When the backup is done, the Windows Backup Has Completed Successfully dialog box appears.

⑮ Click **Close**.

Simplify It

How often should I back up my files?
By default, Windows Backup performs a weekly backup, which is fine for most users. If you use your computer every day to create important business files, you should consider performing backups daily; more occasional users might consider monthly backups. To change the schedule, follow Steps **1** to **4**, click **Change settings**, click **Next**, click **Next**, and then click **Change schedule**.

Can I change my backup configuration?
Yes. Follow Steps **1** to **4** to display the Backup and Restore window, click **Change settings**, and then follow Steps **5** to **9** to adjust your configuration. In the final Set Up Backup dialog box, click **Save settings and exit**.

Restore Backed-Up Files

You can restore a file from a backup if the file is lost because your Windows 7 system crashed, or because the application you used to edit the file had some sort of problem and wrecked the file. You might also need to recover a file if you accidentally overwrote the file or if you deleted it and it was then removed from the Recycle Bin.

Even if you still have the file, you might want to recover an earlier version of it if you improperly edited the file by deleting or changing important data.

Restore Backed-Up Files

1 Click **Start**.

2 Click **All Programs**.

3 Click **Maintenance**.

4 Click **Backup and Restore**.

The Backup and Restore window appears.

5 Click **Restore my files**.

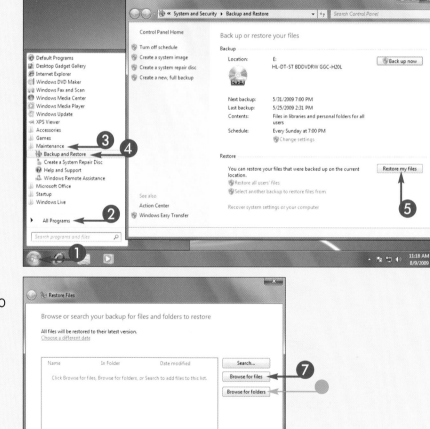

The Browse or Search Your Backup for Files and Folders to Restore dialog box appears.

6 If you backed up using a removable medium such as a CD, DVD, or memory card, insert the medium that contains the backups.

7 Click **Browse for files**.

● If you want to restore an entire folder, click **Browse for folders**, instead.

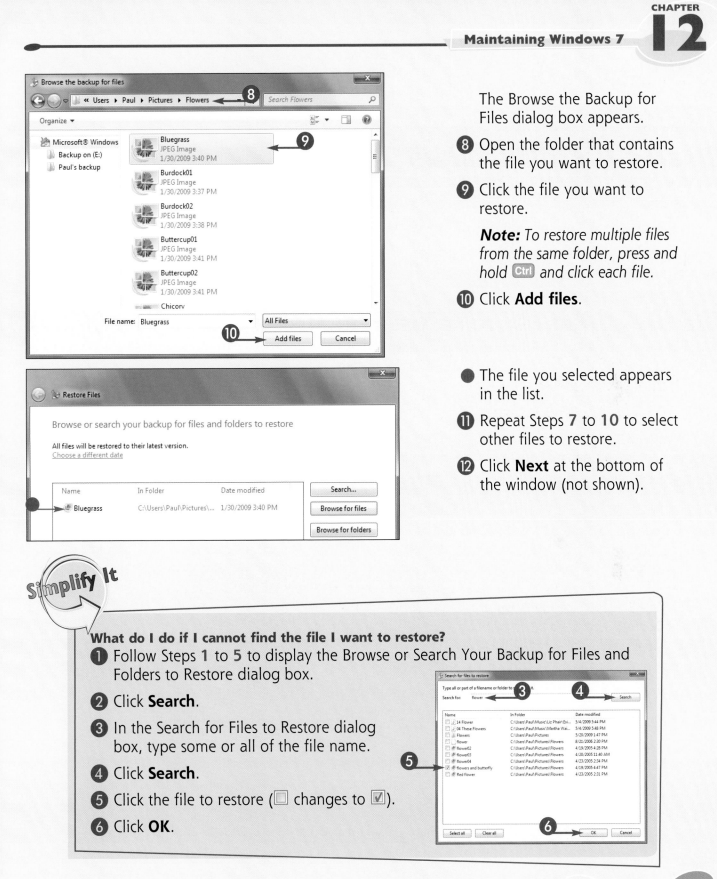

The Browse the Backup for Files dialog box appears.

⑧ Open the folder that contains the file you want to restore.

⑨ Click the file you want to restore.

Note: *To restore multiple files from the same folder, press and hold* Ctrl *and click each file.*

⑩ Click **Add files**.

● The file you selected appears in the list.

⑪ Repeat Steps **7** to **10** to select other files to restore.

⑫ Click **Next** at the bottom of the window (not shown).

Simplify It

What do I do if I cannot find the file I want to restore?

① Follow Steps **1** to **5** to display the Browse or Search Your Backup for Files and Folders to Restore dialog box.

② Click **Search**.

③ In the Search for Files to Restore dialog box, type some or all of the file name.

④ Click **Search**.

⑤ Click the file to restore (☐ changes to ☑).

⑥ Click **OK**.

continued

Restore Backed-Up Files *(continued)*

You can restore all of the backed-up files, which is useful after a major system crash. If you are having problems with or are missing just a few files, you can restore just those backed-up files.

You can also restore the files in their original locations or in a different location. Using a different location is useful if you want to preserve the existing version of a file. By restoring it to a different location, you get to work with both versions.

The Where Do You Want to Restore Your Files? dialog box appears.

⑬ Click **In the original location** (◎ changes to ◉).

● If you prefer to restore the file to another folder, click **In the following location** (◎ changes to ◉), instead, and then click **Browse** to choose the location.

⑭ Click **Restore**.

If you do not have the correct backup media inserted, Windows Backup prompts you to insert the correct disc or drive.

⑮ Insert the requested media.

⑯ Click **OK**.

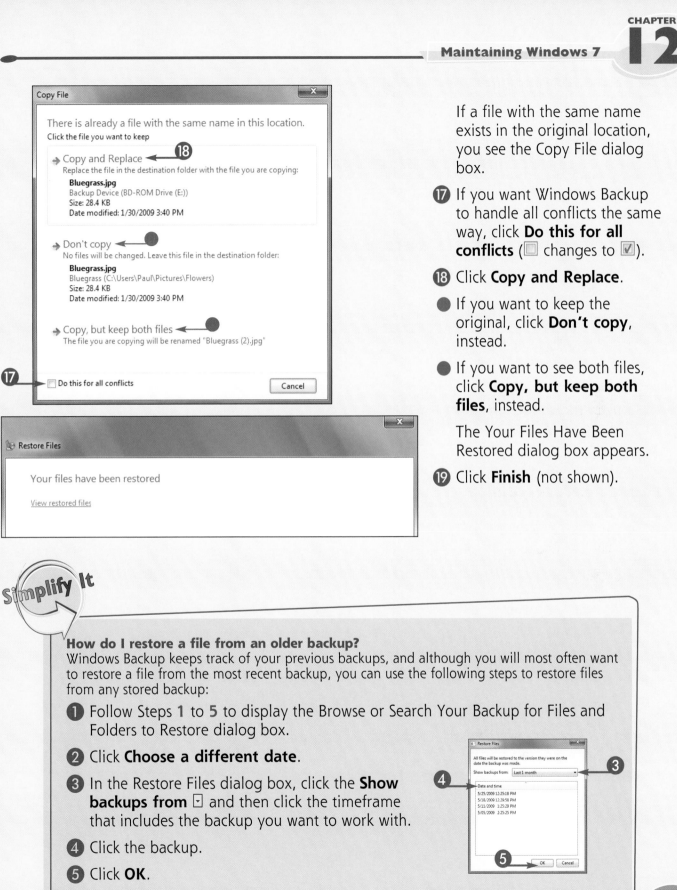

If a file with the same name exists in the original location, you see the Copy File dialog box.

⑰ If you want Windows Backup to handle all conflicts the same way, click **Do this for all conflicts** (☐ changes to ☑).

⑱ Click **Copy and Replace**.

● If you want to keep the original, click **Don't copy**, instead.

● If you want to see both files, click **Copy, but keep both files**, instead.

The Your Files Have Been Restored dialog box appears.

⑲ Click **Finish** (not shown).

Simplify It

How do I restore a file from an older backup?
Windows Backup keeps track of your previous backups, and although you will most often want to restore a file from the most recent backup, you can use the following steps to restore files from any stored backup:

❶ Follow Steps **1** to **5** to display the Browse or Search Your Backup for Files and Folders to Restore dialog box.

❷ Click **Choose a different date**.

❸ In the Restore Files dialog box, click the **Show backups from** ⊡ and then click the timeframe that includes the backup you want to work with.

❹ Click the backup.

❺ Click **OK**.

Index

Index

Index

Index

Index

Read Less–Learn More®

Visual®

There's a Visual book for every learning level...

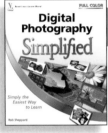

Simplified®

The place to start if you're new to computers. Full color.

- Computers
- Creating Web Pages
- Digital Photography
- Internet
- Mac OS
- Office
- Windows

Teach Yourself VISUALLY™

Get beginning to intermediate-level training in a variety of topics. Full color.

- Access
- Bridge
- Chess
- Computers
- Crocheting
- Digital Photography
- Dog training
- Dreamweaver
- Excel
- Flash
- Golf
- Guitar
- Handspinning
- HTML
- iLife
- iPhoto
- Jewelry Making & Beading
- Knitting
- Mac OS
- Office
- Photoshop
- Photoshop Elements
- Piano
- Poker
- PowerPoint
- Quilting
- Scrapbooking
- Sewing
- Windows
- Wireless Networking
- Word

Top 100 Simplified® Tips & Tricks

Tips and techniques to take your skills beyond the basics. Full color.

- Digital Photography
- eBay
- Excel
- Google
- Internet
- Mac OS
- Office
- Photoshop
- Photoshop Elements
- PowerPoint
- Windows

...all designed for visual learners—just like you!

Master VISUALLY®

Your complete visual reference. Two-color interior.

- 3ds Max
- Creating Web Pages
- Dreamweaver and Flash
- Excel
- Excel VBA Programming
- iPod and iTunes
- Mac OS
- Office
- Optimizing PC Performance
- Photoshop Elements
- QuickBooks
- Quicken
- Windows
- Windows Mobile
- Windows Server

Visual Blueprint™

Where to go for professional-level programming instruction. Two-color interior.

- Ajax
- ASP.NET 2.0
- Excel Data Analysis
- Excel Pivot Tables
- Excel Programming
- HTML
- JavaScript
- Mambo
- PHP & MySQL
- SEO
- Ubuntu Linux
- Vista Sidebar
- Visual Basic
- XML

Visual Encyclopedia™

Your A to Z reference of tools and techniques. Full color.

- Dreamweaver
- Excel
- Mac OS
- Photoshop
- Windows

Visual Quick Tips

Shortcuts, tricks, and techniques for getting more done in less time. Full color.

- Crochet
- Digital Photography
- Excel
- Internet
- iPod & iTunes
- Knitting
- Mac OS
- MySpace
- Office
- PowerPoint
- Windows
- Wireless Networking

Visual®
An Imprint of ⊕WILEY
Now you know.